Day Walks in Loch Lomond & the Trossachs

20 ROUTES IN THE SOUTHERN SCOTTISH HIGHLANDS

Vertebrate Publishing, Sheffield
www.**v-publishing**.co.uk

Day Walks in Loch Lomond & the Trossachs

20 ROUTES IN THE SOUTHERN
SCOTTISH HIGHLANDS

Gerald McGarry

Day Walks in Loch Lomond & the Trossachs

20 ROUTES IN THE SOUTHERN
SCOTTISH HIGHLANDS

VP First published in 2021 by Vertebrate Publishing.

Vertebrate Publishing, Omega Court, 352 Cemetery Road,
Sheffield S11 8FT, United Kingdom.
www.v-publishing.co.uk

Copyright © 2021 Gerald McGarry and Vertebrate Publishing Ltd.

Gerald McGarry has asserted his rights under the Copyright, Designs
and Patents Act 1988 to be identified as author of this work.

A CIP catalogue record for this book is available from the British Library.

ISBN 978-1-83981-071-8

All rights reserved. No part of this work covered by the copyright herein may be reproduced or used
in any form or by any means – graphic, electronic, or mechanised, including photocopying, recording,
taping, or information storage and retrieval systems – without the written permission of the publisher.

Front cover: **The Cobbler** (*route 10*).
Back cover: **Avoiding bogs near The Whangie** (*route 3*).
Photography by Gerald McGarry unless otherwise credited.

All maps reproduced by permission of Ordnance Survey on
behalf of The Controller of Her Majesty's Stationery Office.
© Crown Copyright. 100025218.

Design by Jane Beagley, production by Cameron Bonser.
www.v-publishing.co.uk

Printed and bound in Europe by Pulsio.

Vertebrate Publishing is committed to printing on paper from sustainable sources.

MIX
Paper from
responsible sources
FSC® C128169

Every effort has been made to achieve accuracy of the information in this guidebook. The authors, publishers and copyright
owners can take no responsibility for: loss or injury (including fatal) to persons; loss or damage to property or equipment;
trespass, irresponsible behaviour or any other mishap that may be suffered as a result of following the route descriptions
or advice offered in this guidebook. The inclusion of a track or path as part of a route, or otherwise recommended, in this
guidebook does not guarantee that the track or path will remain a right of way. If conflict with landowners arises we advise
that you act politely and leave by the shortest route available. If the matter needs to be taken further then please take it up
with the relevant authority.

Contents

Loch Lomond & the Trossachs
Area Map & Route Finder vi
Introduction ix
Acknowledgements x
About the walks x
Navigation x
GPS & mobile phones xi
Walk times xi
Safety xi
Clothing, equipment and some hazards xii
Scottish Outdoor Access Code xii
Livestock xiii
Stalking xiii
Flora and fauna xiv
How to use this book xv
Maps, descriptions, distances xvi
Km/mile conversion chart xvi

SECTION 1 – Loch Lomond South

1. Conic Hill **3.7km** 5
2. Ben Lomond **11.4km** 9
3. The Whangie & Auchineden Hill **4.4km** 15
4. Dumgoyne **3km** 19
5. Northern Luss Hills **18.4km** 23

SECTION 2 – The Trossachs

6. Ben Venue **13.3km** 33
7. Ben Ledi **9.9km** 39
8. Ben A'an **3.8km** 43

SECTION 3 – Arrochar Alps

9. Cruach Tairbeirt **4.1km** 51
10. The Cobbler **10.9km** 55
11. Beinn an Lochain **4.7km** 61
12. Glen Loin & the Sloy Dam **21.9km** 67
13. Ben Donich **6.6km** 73
14. The Brack **6.9km** 77
15. Ben Vane **11.2km** 81
16. Cnoc Coinnich & The Steeple **9.8km** 87
17. Beinn Narnain **11.8km** 93

SECTION 4 – The Northern Hills

18. Ben More & Stob Binnein **9.6km** 103
19. An Caisteal **10.5km** 109
20. Ben Vorlich & Stùc a'Chroin **14.2km** 115

APPENDIX 120

VIEW FROM THE BRACK (ROUTE 14)
© FRASER MCGARRY

Loch Lomond South

1. Conic Hill **3.7km** 5
2. Ben Lomond **11.4km** 9
3. The Whangie & Auchineden Hill **4.4km** .. 15
4. Dumgoyne **3km** 19
5. Northern Luss Hills **18.4km** 23

The Trossachs

6. Ben Venue **13.3km** 33
7. Ben Ledi **9.9km** 39
8. Ben A'an **3.8km** 43

Arrochar Alps

9. Cruach Tairbeirt **4.1km** 51
10. The Cobbler **10.9km** 55
11. Beinn an Lochain **4.7km** 61
12. Glen Loin & the Sloy Dam **21.9km** 67
13. Ben Donich **6.6km** 73
14. The Brack **6.9km** 77
15. Ben Vane **11.2km** 81
16. Cnoc Coinnich & The Steeple **9.8km** ... 87
17. Beinn Narnain **11.8km** 93

The Northern Hills

18. Ben More & Stob Binnein **9.6km** 103
19. An Caisteal **10.5km** 109
20. Ben Vorlich & Stùc a'Chroin **14.2km** ... 115

Day Walks in Loch Lomond & the Trossachs

AREA MAP & ROUTE FINDER

AREA MAP & ROUTE FINDER vii

CRAGS ON BEN VENUE (ROUTE 6)

Introduction

The mountains, lochs and forests of Loch Lomond and the Trossachs have attracted walkers and outdoors enthusiasts for generations. The importance of this area due to its natural beauty and biodiversity led in 2002 to it becoming Scotland's first national park. However, do not let the word 'park' fool you. True, the land has been tamed with paths and signposts on the popular routes, but if you are 1,000 metres up on Ben More in a storm then you will know this is not a 'walk in the park'.

Loch Lomond & the Trossachs National Park covers around 1,865 square kilometres of stunning landscape, all within one hour's drive for half of the population of Scotland. The area contains 21 Munros, 19 Corbetts and a multitude of smaller hills, long-distance paths and cycle routes – there is enough to last a lifetime for walkers, climbers and water sports enthusiasts.

The scope for walking and exploration in the magnificent Loch Lomond and Trossachs is almost infinite, and our little list of day walks only just scratches the surface of what is available in the region. Today, more than ever, society is becoming aware of the health and well-being benefits of walking in the wild, outdoor spaces of our countryside. As more people take to the hills the environmental impacts of increased visitor pressure are being felt throughout the national park. Car parks fill up early, litter has become a major problem in some areas and path erosion has accelerated in recent years. Many of our walks are very popular so it is a good idea to go early or at off-peak times, and if car parks are full then just go somewhere else rather than parking irresponsibly.

Our selected walks are all easily achievable in a day or half day. They range from low-level paths to strenuous outings in the high mountains and most are on clear, well-trodden trails through stunning scenery. So let's get our boots on and head for the hills!

Gerald McGarry

Acknowledgements

I am grateful to my regular walking companions, especially Carol McGarry, Fraser McGarry and Murray Wilkie, for putting up with my many photo stops. Thanks also go to the many walkers who allowed me to take their photo when I was out walking alone. Thanks also to the team at Vertebrate Publishing who kept me right!

About the walks

The walks in this book range between 1.9 and 13.6 miles (3 and 21.9 kilometres) and will take around two and a half to eight hours at average walking speed without allowing for stops.

This is a rugged and mountainous region, and the walks reflect that. None of the walks are signed or waymarked throughout, so some map reading ability is essential. Be prepared for some pathless terrain requiring good navigation skills, particularly in poor weather. For the mountain walks, previous hillwalking experience is assumed.

Navigation

The walks are laid out with detailed, easily followed steps, but the book is ideally used alongside a map and compass. Paper maps allow the walker to study the route in advance and make sense of the descriptions in the book. For most of the walks compass work is unlikely to be needed on a clear day but having a map and compass (along with the ability to use them) will come in handy when the cloud comes down and the path disappears. Some key grid references are included but compass bearings have not been provided as these are generally not needed.

The routes in this book are covered by the following maps in the OS 1:25,000 Explorer series:

348 Campsie Fells
OL37 Cowal East
OL38 Loch Lomond South
OL39 Loch Lomond North
OL46 The Trossachs

Harvey Maps produce the excellent *Loch Lomond & the Trossachs National Park Outdoor Atlas* (1:40,000), which covers almost all the walks in this book.

GPS and mobile phones

A GPS device is always useful. If this is on a mobile phone carry a powerpack to prevent the battery from going flat. Smartphones are particularly useful if an emergency arises as it can aid rescuers in locating the phone's position if a signal is present. However, do not rely on having mobile phone signal.

Walk times

Walk times are approximate; allow extra time for breaks and to explore places of interest along the way. If a walk goes off path across moorland this can add time; in winter always allow extra time.

Safety

Before beginning any of these walks it is important to ensure you are fully prepared for changeable conditions both in terms of weather and underfoot. Having the correct clothing and equipment is crucial, and you should always be fully prepared for any adverse or emergency situations. Leave details of your route with a person who knows what to do if you have not returned by a certain time.

The emergency services are there if you need them, but being wet, tired or hungry is not a reason to summon them. In summer conditions most people can get themselves back to safety unless injured, even after dark. However, if you are lost, on steep ground and are unable to make safe progress it may be time to call someone before an injury happens!

RESCUE

In case of an emergency dial **999** and ask for **Police** and then **Mountain Rescue**. Where possible give a six-figure grid reference of your location or that of your casualty. If you don't have mobile reception try to attract the attention of others nearby. The standard distress signal is six short blasts on a whistle every minute.

EMERGENCY RESCUE BY SMS TEXT

In the UK you can also contact the emergency services by SMS text – useful if you have low battery or intermittent signal. You need to register your phone first by texting '**register**' to **999** and then following the instructions in the reply. Do it now – it could save yours or someone else's life. **www.emergencysms.net**

Clothing, equipment and some hazards

All of the walks are described for a summer outing. Snow on any of the high-level walks transforms them into a mountaineering expedition. In winter the seriousness of these hills should not be underestimated; ice axe, crampons and full mountaineering equipment should be the norm. For our purposes we are assuming a nice summer's day.

The walks require no specialist equipment beyond that which every hillwalker should possess. A pair of walking boots with stiff soles and deep treads is essential. Synthetic fibres are ideal for trousers and top layers as they hold warmth even when wet and they dry quickly. A waterproof jacket and an additional warm layer should always be carried. Walking poles help with balance on steep paths and are invaluable for stream crossings.

Long trousers and long-sleeved tops are recommended given the recent increase in Lyme disease. Ticks are most often encountered in bracken and heather, so keep on the path and don't lie down for a rest in the bracken! Lighter coloured clothing makes it easy to see the pests if they land on you! Use a tick removal tool if needed.

On windless, overcast days we may encounter the occasional midge. The Highland midge is the scourge of the region; forming squadrons of several million, they can reduce a grown walker to tears. Fortunately, there is often a breeze (or to be honest a howling gale) to keep them away, but be warned, once you stop, they can be a major menace. Use midge repellent liberally on 'midgey' days. You have been warned.

Scottish Outdoor Access Code
See **www.outdooraccess-scotland.scot** for more details.

TAKE RESPONSIBILITY FOR YOUR OWN ACTIONS
» Care for your own safety
» Keep alert for hazards
» Take special care with children

RESPECT PEOPLE'S PRIVACY AND PEACE OF MIND
» Do not act in ways that might annoy or alarm people, especially at night

HELP LAND MANAGERS AND OTHERS TO WORK SAFELY AND EFFECTIVELY
» Keep clear of land management operations like harvesting or tree-felling
» Avoid damaging crops
» Leave gates as you find them

CARE FOR YOUR ENVIRONMENT
» Don't disturb wildlife
» Take your litter away with you

KEEP YOUR DOG UNDER PROPER CONTROL
» Take special care if near livestock or during the bird breeding season
» Always pick up after your dog

Livestock

Hill farming is an important part of the rural economy. On most of our hills we will encounter sheep and on many we may get closer than we would like to cattle, occasionally the ginger, hairy variety with big horns. Much of the issue here is a result of the interaction between dogs and livestock. Dogs can do a lot of damage to sheep, especially during lambing, so keep man's best friend on a leash. Cattle can present a real hazard to walkers and recently there have been fatalities. In general, keep away from cows; if possible do not enter a field with cattle in it. Sometimes cattle graze on open hillsides and may even be right on the path. Give them as much space as possible and never get between a cow and its calf. If they charge do not run but back off keeping a close eye on them.

Stalking

Scotland's Highland estates rely on deer stalking for income and the culling of red deer is essential to minimise the damage that they do to the upland environment. Most of the shooting takes place from 1 July until 20 October, with peak activity from August onwards. In general, sticking to paths and accepted hill routes is sufficient to avoid disturbing the stalkers. During the stalking season it is worth checking **www.outdooraccess-scotland.scot/practical-guide-all/heading-scottish-hills** for any activity in the area where you're planning to walk.

Flora and fauna

When walking we tend to look upwards, but sometimes looking down and more closely at the details beside the path reveals wonderful flowers, insects and plants. Bog cotton, speckled orchids, bluebells, pink and purple cushions of alpine saxifrage, wild garlic, sorrel and anemones are all common to the region.

You may be lucky enough to see an adder, a slow worm (which looks like a snake but is a legless lizard) or a common lizard; one even scuttled over my hand one day when I was rock climbing on Ben A'an.

Red deer and the smaller roe deer are common; on still autumn days the bellowing of rutting stags echoes around the corries. Mountain hares and ptarmigan are easily spotted in winter due to their white coats making them stand out when the snows are late to arrive.

Golden eagles are often confused with buzzards (tourist eagles) but once you have seen an eagle you won't make the buzzard mistake again. In summer, osprey live in the region and are commonly spotted around Loch Lomond itself. Ravens are intelligent birds and often hang around summit areas mooching for scraps of food from walkers.

On forest approaches it is a good idea to walk quietly then you might be lucky to see red squirrels, pine marten or maybe a badger. Great spotted woodpecker, owls, nuthatch, tree creepers and bullfinch are common in the woodland areas of the national park. In the faster flowing rivers, the iconic little black and white dipper can be seen hunting for insect larvae. Keep your eyes wide open, walk quietly through the forests and don't forget to look down as well as up.

How to use this book

This book should provide you with all of the information that you need for an enjoyable, trouble-free and successful walk. The following tips should also be of help:

» We strongly recommend that you invest in the relevant OS map for the walk. These are essential even if you are familiar with the area – you may need to cut short the walk or take an alternative route.
» Choose your route. Consider the time you have available and the abilities and level of experience of all members of your party – then read the Safety section of this guidebook.
» We recommend that you study the route description carefully before setting off. Cross-reference this with your map so that you've got a good sense of general orientation in case you need an escape route. Make sure that you are familiar with the symbols used on the maps.
» Get out there and get walking!

ON THE LOCH LOMOND AND COWAL WAY (ROUTE 12)

Maps, descriptions, distances

While every effort has been made to maintain accuracy within the maps and descriptions in this guidebook, we have had to process a vast amount of information and we are unable to guarantee that every single detail is correct. Please exercise caution if a direction appears at odds with the route on the map. If in doubt, a comparison between the route, the description and a quick cross-reference with your map (along with a bit of common sense) should help ensure that you're on the right track.

Note that distances have been measured off the map, and map distances rarely coincide 100 per cent with distances on the ground. Please treat stated distances as a guideline only. Ordnance Survey maps are the most commonly used, are easy to read and many people are happy using them. If you're not familiar with OS maps and are unsure of what the symbols mean, you can download a free OS 1:25,000 map legend from **www.ordnancesurvey.co.uk**

Here are a few of the symbols and abbreviations we use on the maps and in our directions:

ROUTE STARTING POINT	SHORTCUT	ROUTE MARKER	OPTIONAL ROUTE	ADDITIONAL GRID LINE NUMBERS TO AID NAVIGATION

KM/MILE CONVERSION CHART

Metric to Imperial
1 kilometre [km]	1,000 m	0.6214 mile
1 metre [m]	100 cm	1.0936 yd
1 centimetre [cm]	10 mm	0.3937 in
1 millimetre [mm]		0.03937 in

Imperial to Metric
1 mile	1,760 yd	1.6093 km
1 yard [yd]	3 ft	0.9144 m
1 foot [ft]	12 in	0.3048 m
1 inch [in]		2.54 cm

TRIG POINT ON THE BRACK (ROUTE 14)

Section 1

Loch Lomond South

The wide southern basin of Loch Lomond straddles the Highland Boundary Fault. Here we see the transition from low rolling hills and farmland to wilder more rugged mountain terrain. This area of the national park is studded with small villages and offers the walker everything from gentle walks and short hill days to more strenuous climbs. The challenges culminate in the ascent of Scotland's most southerly Munro, the mighty Ben Lomond.

DUMGOYNE (ROUTE 4)

LOOKING SOUTH-EAST FROM BEINN EICH (ROUTE 5)

LOCH LOMOND & THE TROSSACHS – SECTION 1

ON THE DESCENT FROM CONIC HILL

01 Conic Hill

3.7km/2.3 miles

Walk the line between the Lowlands and the Highlands.

Balmaha » Bealach Ard » Conic Hill » Bealach Ard » Balmaha

Start
Balmaha car park; often very busy.
GR: NS 421909.

The Walk
Like its southerly neighbour, Dumgoyne, this little hill punches way above its weight. Viewed from almost any direction (except perhaps one) Conic Hill has nothing conical about it. Its name is an Anglicisation of *Coinneach*, meaning mossy mountain. So, it is not conical and it is not a particularly mossy hill either, but it is a lovely little viewpoint above the southern basin of Loch Lomond.

Conic Hill sits squat and defiant right on top of the Highland Boundary Fault. This geological fault line runs south-west to north-east across Scotland, separating the Lowlands from the Highlands. On Conic Hill looking to the south we can see the flat plains of the Midland Valley, with low, gentle rolling hills, such as the Campsie Fells and Kilpatrick Hills. The rocks of this lowland region are mainly soft sandstones that were easily worn down by the glaciers. To the north it is a different scene: towering, jagged mountains formed of harder schists and granites. These fire- and pressure-formed rocks refused to be worn down by the great glaciers and that is partly why they are the Highlands and the softer rocks are the Lowlands.

On today's walk the geology is laid out before us. Conglomerates, where soft sandstone has had dense rocky pebbles imbedded within it, are obvious once you know where to look. Looking north, Loch Lomond is a narrow fjord, where the glaciers had to squeeze through the hard rocks. To the south the loch is wide and shallow; the glaciers had an easier time here, spreading out on the softer bedrock and depositing their cargo of stones and silt. On the summit look to the south-west and see the islands of the southern basin of the loch lined up perfectly along the fault line. Seeing this, we realise that Conic Hill is just another island, one that put up a fight and refused to be totally worn down. Although Conic Hill is geologically of the Lowlands, its heart is in the Highlands!

CONIC HILL
DISTANCE: 3.7KM/2.3 MILES » **TOTAL ASCENT**: 303M/994FT » **START GR**: NS 421909 » **TIME**: ALLOW 3 HOURS **SATNAV**: G63 0JQ » **MAP**: OS EXPLORER OL38, LOCH LOMOND SOUTH, 1:25,000 » **REFRESHMENTS**: OAK TREE INN, BALMAHA » **NAVIGATION**: STRAIGHTFORWARD.

Directions – Conic Hill

S Leave the car park at its north-east edge near a signpost for the *Balmaha Millennium Forest Path*. The path winds through a forest of birch trees, much favoured by the dreaded midge. After 300m **turn left** at a junction and continue up a steeper path. The forest changes quite suddenly to tall, mighty pines. Go up a staircase to a swing gate and our first view of the upper hill.

2 Beyond the gate the nature of the path changes again. The forest thins out as we climb steeply up and round to the **left** on stone steps through lovely rowan trees (mountain ash). Near the top of the steps, we cross our first good example of conglomerate (the geological equivalent of 'fruit and nut' chocolate). Move up and **right** for a breather at a muddy, flatter section. Head up **stone steps, steeply to the right**, to reach the Bealach Ard. Take a moment here to enjoy our first views of Loch Lomond, its islands and the Highlands beyond ... super!

3 The broad path climbs up and **right** (north-east). **Ignore** a faint path going steeply up to the right. Continue until the main path leads up to the **right**, through a band of rock towards the summit. Be careful on the final section as the giant pebbles of the conglomerate are very slippery. The summit is a broad dome – no cairn or trig point – but we can still take some time to enjoy the views. To the north, we can see Ben Lomond; the Trossachs are obscured by the eastern shoulder of the Ben. Moving clockwise, to the east are the Ochil Hills and on a clear day the National Wallace Monument in Stirling is visible. Further round and closer to us are Stronend near Fintry and the northern escarpment of the Campsie Fells, with flat tops and deep glacier-gouged corries. Continuing to the south-east we can see Dumgoyne, then the Blane Valley, Glasgow and, in the distance, Tinto, far to the south. Turning west, we see the Kilpatrick Hills and Duncolm. Below us, Endrick Water snakes into the loch at Endrick Mouth, just south of Balmaha. The River Leven, the outflow of Loch Lomond, lies south-west of the lined-up islands on the loch. In the distance are the mountains of Arran and then, in the west, the Luss Hills lead in a crescendo to the Arrochar Alps. The Cobbler is easily spotted and then over the summit of Ptarmigan and back to our start, Ben Lomond.

4 To descend we **retrace our steps** enjoying the fine open views to the islands and loch. Once back at Bealach Ard, **walk south-west for 200m** to a flat area with great views. Once satisfied, go **left** down a path to regain the main track. Once back at the car park, take the opportunity to visit the Tom Weir statue, close to the bay. Tom Weir was a legendary Glaswegian hillwalker, mountaineer, climber, naturalist and author. His 1970s and 1980s television programmes inspired a generation of Scots to take to the hills. He lived locally and frequented the same hills that we are exploring in this little book. The statue is a good likeness, and I am sure he would have had a thing or two to tell us about Conic Hill and the Highland Boundary Fault!

Notes: This walk could be a circuit, descending the south-west ridge to the roadside north of the Pass of Balmaha. However, this entails crossing farmland used for grazing and then a narrow section of busy road.

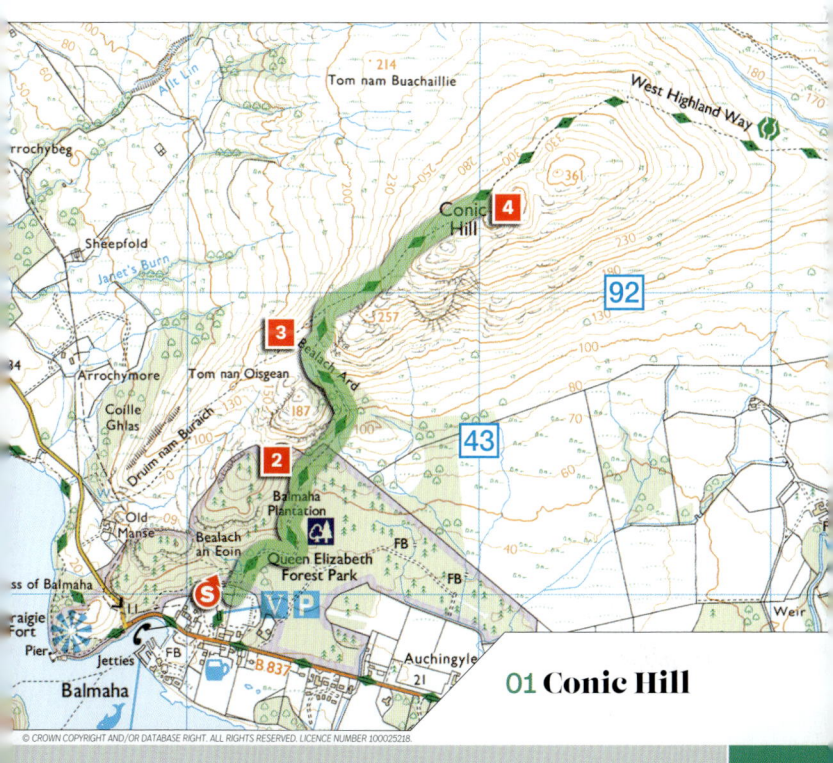

01 Conic Hill

LOOKING DOWN THE NORTH-WEST RIDGE

02 Ben Lomond   11.4km/7.1 miles

A spectacular circuit of Scotland's most southerly Munro.

Rowardennan » Ptarmigan path » Ptarmigan summit » Ben Lomond north-west ridge » Ben Lomond summit » Tourist path » Rowardennan

Start
Ben Lomond car park, Rowardennan (parking charge). GR: NS 360986. In summer a ferry operates from Tarbet.

The Walk
Lying close to the Central Belt population centres, Ben Lomond (Beacon Mountain) is Scotland's most southerly and most popular Munro. The 'Ben', clearly visible from their city, is for many Glaswegians the only mountain they will ever climb. Tens of thousands hike to the summit every year, many in shorts, t-shirts, trainers or flip-flops, via the broad 'tourist track' from Rowardennan on the bonnie banks of Loch Lomond.

Despite the indignity of the hoards, this is a real mountain, 974 metres high with steep summit slopes, a precipitous rocky corrie on its northern side and long gentle slopes on its south-west flank. When the weather turns bad, as it often does, things can get serious and the gentle slopes of the tourist track make it difficult to get down quickly. The Ben can be an exposed place to be caught out in t-shirt and shorts!

The north-west ridge is known as the Ptarmigan Ridge as it climbs up over the subsidiary summit named after that sturdy little high-altitude grouse. Our route uses this ridge to traverse the mountain and then we descend by the tourist track. The north-west ridge gains interest with height, and the final 300 metres are steep and quite narrow. The finale is an easy pull on to the very top with the trig pillar suddenly appearing at eye level. Views are tremendous in all directions. While the Ben is seldom a solitary experience, especially in high summer, it is a big enough mountain to allow us to escape the crowds. So, let's enjoy our climb up this most touristic of mountains and let's see how many ill-equipped ascensionists we can spot!

BEN LOMOND
DISTANCE: 11.4KM/7.1 MILES » **TOTAL ASCENT**: 962M/3,156FT » **START GR**: NS 360986 » **TIME**: ALLOW 6 HOURS
SATNAV: G63 0AR » **MAP**: OS EXPLORER OL39, LOCH LOMOND NORTH, 1:25,000 » **REFRESHMENTS**: ROWARDENNAN HOTEL » **NAVIGATION**: STRAIGHTFORWARD.

ARROCHAR AND BEN LOMOND AT SUNRISE

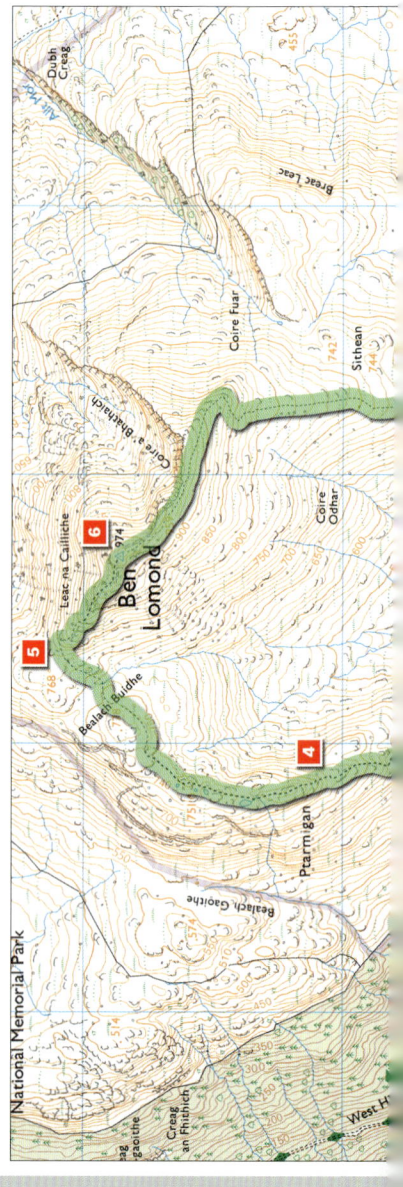

02 **Ben Lomond**

02 BEN LOMOND – LOCH LOMOND SOUTH

Directions – Ben Lomond

S Leave the car park heading **north** along the broad track past a circular stone monument at the lochside. **Ignore** a turn off left that leads to a youth hostel and another on the right leading to houses. Pass a white cottage on our right where it is sometimes possible to buy bottled water at an honesty stand. Cross a low footbridge and arrive at a signpost (to *Ptarmigan*) at the start of the path to the north-west ridge route (NS 359995).

2 **Turn right** along the path. The path winds steeply up through the woodland, goes through a gate then zigzags upwards. After a broad, boggy area the path swings to the **left** across the western slopes of Tom Fithich. Views to the western shore of Loch Lomond open up below.

3 **Cross a burn** and then go through a swing gate. The path levels before arriving at the foot of the steeper slopes up to Ptarmigan. On our left, before the first zigzag of the path, is a flat boulder, a good place for a breather and to take in the views to the southern end of the loch with its myriad of islands. The well-defined path climbs steeply up the side of Ptarmigan before levelling out and crossing the summit of this western outlier of Ben Lomond (NN 358022; 731m).

4 Continue **straight ahead**. A photogenic lochan is passed with views to the north and west before the path swings to the **north-east** and descends to a col with large stepping stones across a bog. This is the start of the final ridge leading directly to the summit of Ben Lomond.

5 The path turns **south-east** and climbs steeply in a series of bends through rocky ground. Initially broad, the ridge becomes narrower with height. To our left lies the north face and to our right the eye is drawn to the islands of the southern end of Loch Lomond and across to the Luss Hills. Careful footwork is required around numerous small rocky steps, places where a slip could go a long way! Near the top the path goes between two large boulders (the Pearly Gates) before heading steeply to a final easy rocky scramble which sees us pop over the edge, eyes level with the summit trig point – a dramatic finish to a splendid ridge.

6 The summit (NN 367028; 974m) is a place to linger and enjoy the 360-degree views. To the north, the Crianlarich Hills, Ben Lui and, on a clear day, the Glencoe Hills are easily spotted. To the east we can see the Trossachs, Ben Ledi, Ben Venue and the Ochil Hills. To the south we have Dumgoyne, the Campsie Fells and the Southern Uplands. But it is the vistas to the west and north-west that capture most people's attention, with Loch Lomond providing a perfect foreground for the Luss Hills and across the to the Arrochar Alps. To start the descent, follow the path **south-east** along the summit ridge, stopping from time to time to look over to the left at the cliffs of the northern corrie, the location of some short technical winter climbs. The path swings to the **right**, heading south down a broad, open slope. At the foot of this slope a large cairn marks the start of the long gradual, plateau section leading down to Sròn Aonaich at 577m.

7 The long descent is compensated by fine open views of the loch and islands far below. After passing through a gate a steeper descent leads across a footbridge then down through the forest to the car park.

Notes: this is a very popular hill so expect the path and the car park to be busy. Accidents are frequent here due to poorly prepared walkers underestimating the challenge. In winter this is a mountaineering route, which can be totally unrecognisable from its summer state.

BEN LOMOND AND THE FULL MOON

THE GENDARME

03 The Whangie & Auchineden Hill — 4.4km/2.7 miles

A trip to a geological marvel and a viewpoint worthy of Auld Nick.

Queen's View » The Whangie » Auchineden Hill » Queen's View

Start
Queen's View and The Whangie car park. GR: NS 511808.

The Walk
This walk lies just beyond the southern boundary of the national park, but it has earned inclusion for its splendid views and entertainment value. Auchineden Hill is often incorrectly referred to as 'The Whangie', a title that belongs to the strange geological formation located on the northern slopes of the hill. Many set out for The Whangie, follow the path system to the summit and miss the highlight of the walk entirely. We won't miss out; we will head for the summit only after we have fully explored the weird rock formations hidden below the trig point.

The Whangie has a special place in the history of rock climbing in the region and used to be busy on summer evenings. Indoor climbing walls, with music, coffee, warmth and a feeling of guaranteed safety have led to its sad demise as a trad climbing venue. The bizarre rock formations consist of inner and outer cliffs, separated by a deep narrow cleft, and eroded into pinnacles and cracks. The Gendarme is encountered before the main crag or 'flake'. Look around the outside of the cliffs then go inside and along the chasm. As we explore, it is worth thinking about how it was formed. The clue is in the name as *whang* means a whipcrack! Legend says that the Devil, late for a meeting with witches in nearby Carbeth, flew over Auchineden Hill, flicked his tail and with a mighty devilish whang, split the rocks. Obviously, this is the most likely cause of the rock split, but some try to explain it using science. Of many possible explanations, the most logical is that the glaciers sheared the basalt cliff creating the split we see today. This seems likely as the inner and outer walls look as if they could be fitted back together like a giant jigsaw.

Once we have explored the rocks continue around to the summit for fantastic views in all directions. On the descent we cross an elevated bog that will soak you with mud to the knees for sure, a real sting in the tail!

THE WHANGIE & AUCHINEDEN HILL

DISTANCE: 4.4KM/2.7 MILES » **TOTAL ASCENT**: 172M/564FT » **START GR**: NS 511808 » **TIME**: ALLOW 2.5-3 HOURS **SATNAV**: G63 9QL » **MAP**: OS EXPLORER OL38, LOCH LOMOND SOUTH, 1:25,000 » **REFRESHMENTS**: ST MOCHA DRIVE THRU, CARBETH » **NAVIGATION**: OBVIOUS PATH SYSTEM BUT POSSIBILITY OF TAKING A WRONG TURN AND MISSING THE WHANGIE IF ROUTE NOT CAREFULLY FOLLOWED.

Directions – The Whangie & Auchineden Hill

S➤ Queen's View was named following a visit by Queen Victoria when she had her first glimpse of Loch Lomond and was most amused. Leave the parking area at the south-west corner and cross the wall on to the boardwalk across the bog (more of this later!). Go uphill, through a gate then go **right** up the broad slope. Views are already good but you 'ain't seen nothing yet'. At the top of this first rise the path levels off. At a ruined fence a path climbs steeply upwards to the left, we will return this way. For now, go **straight ahead** (west). After about 1km **ignore** the path going up and to the left (this is where most people go wrong). Continue **straight ahead**, with more ups and downs and some more mud. Eventually the trail trends left and we start to see some rocks.

2 The first rocks to appear are the Gendarme, French for policeman, a term applied in alpinism for a pinnacle guarding a ridge. Walk around the Gendarme. The inside face is smooth and polished by the feet and hands of generations of rock climbers. Climb down a small rocky step and walk along the outside of the main flake. The crag towers above us until at a third of the way along there is a lower point between two pinnacles – we will return here from within the chasm. The views to the north are of the entire southern basin of Loch Lomond. At the extreme western end of the main flake look for a steep path going upwards and **left**, this is the entry point to the chasm of The Whangie. As soon as we enter the split, we can see that the smooth walls are the reciprocal of each other, it is as if we could go outside and push them back together. Continue to the low balcony, looking north over the loch through a picture frame of rock pillars. The chasm now descends to exit at the Gendarme. Go back to the most south-west end of the main flake and follow the path up and **left** across a broad slope to a small bealach. Go up and **right** here and we can see the trig point just up ahead.

3 The trig point sits on a small rocky slab. The views are incredible for such a low elevation. To the north, Conic Hill is immediately obvious. Turning clockwise we can see Ben Venue and then the Kippen Flats and the sharp edge of Stronend. To the east is Dumgoyne then, continuing to turn clockwise, we can see the Slackdhu escarpment above the Blane Valley. In the distance (south-south-west) lies the pointed summit of Tinto. To the south we are looking at the Clyde Valley and Glasgow; if it is late afternoon, late in the year, the lights will be coming on … magical. In the west we can see Duncolm, the highest point of the Kilpatrick Hills, and

Cochno Hill. The Luss Hills, the islands of the south of Loch Lomond and then mighty Ben Lomond bring us home. The view is so good we might just go around again!

4 So, we have had fun exploring but as the saying goes, there's 'nowt for nowt', it's time to pay. Start the descent by heading **north-east** on a broad track and immediately cross a deep swamp. If we get it wrong here, we will be practising the breaststroke; take a wide arc and rejoin the path. There is a choice of paths; the **right-hand path is best** as it stays high for longer. Cross a small fore-summit with a low cairn. Beyond the cairn are more bogs and swamps but in general, **keep right**, heading towards the telephone mast up ahead. Follow a broad, muddy path down and **left** until we can join a faint path heading **right** towards the forestry plantation. Now turn **sharp left** and descend to the ruined fence, then **turn right** to return to the car park.

Notes: Could be walked in either direction. The summit could also be climbed without The Whangie; but, honestly, why would you do such a thing?

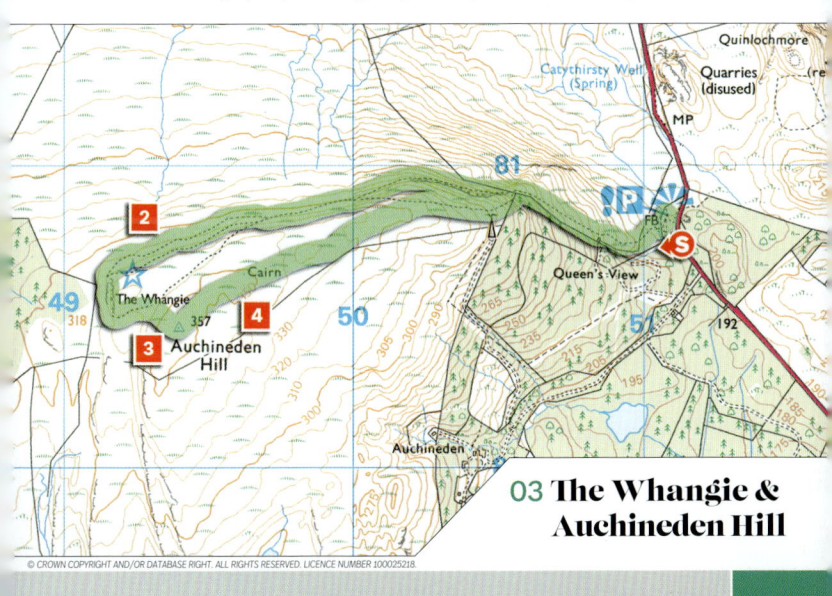

03 **The Whangie & Auchineden Hill**

ON THE DESCENT FROM DUMGOYNE

04 Dumgoyne

3km/1.9 miles

A short, steep, stiff climb to a spectacular viewpoint on the edge of the national park. A cask-strength miniature!

Glengoyne Distillery » Dumgoyne » Glengoyne Distillery

Start
Glengoyne Distillery. GR: NS 527827. Parking available in a small lay-by on the A81 just to the north of Glengoyne Distillery. Do not park in the distillery car park (gates are locked after business hours).

The Walk
What this striking little mountain lacks in altitude it more than makes up for in attitude. Dumgoyne means 'fort of the arrowhead'. Clearly it was a perfect defensive summit for ancient inhabitants. Poking out defiantly from the north-west extremity of the Campsie Fells, this excrescence of volcanic rock is all that remains of a once much bigger mountain. Ground down by ancient glaciers, this volcanic plug forced them to turn around its rocky core. There is visible evidence of its volcanic origin high up on the hillside.

There are many ways to climb Dumgoyne, but our route is in keeping with the feisty character of the hill: a direct straight-up frontal assault. Pick a good day for this short outing, it is popular so go early. Early on a clear morning is ideal, when the cloud still hangs in the valley and the air is cool for the climb. Better still, go late. Late in the year and late in the day. An autumnal evening, when the hill is quiet, and, as the sun sinks behind the Kilpatrick Hills, the streetlights of Glasgow are twinkling below to the south. Magical, but bring a torch for the tricky descent.

DUMGOYNE

DISTANCE: 3KM/1.9 MILES » **TOTAL ASCENT**: 370M/1,214FT » **START GR**: NS 527827 » **TIME**: ALLOW 2.5–3 HOURS
SATNAV: G63 9LB » **MAP**: OS EXPLORER 348, CAMPSIE FELLS, 1:25,000 » **REFRESHMENTS**: BEECH TREE INN, DUMGOYNE » **NAVIGATION**: SIMPLE, WIDE OBVIOUS PATH. NARROW SECTION NEEDS CARE.

Directions – Dumgoyne

S From the front gates of the distillery go into the field just to the south (on the **right**). **Cross the stile and walk east** on the broad path, which slopes gently upwards. Sheep graze here and on the upper hillside so keep dogs on a lead. We pass an array of solar panels to our left and head straight for the front (western aspect) of the upper hill.

2 **Cross a track** and enter the upper field. Follow the wide, grassy path upwards between a pair of trees and around a fallen tree that was blown over years ago and continues to grow – resilience! The path leads to two parallel fences with rickety stiles enclosing a mere trickle of a burn. **Cross these fences and the burn** and arrive at a muddy area below the main hill. Looking upwards you will see a path to our left (heading north) and a more direct path straight ahead and slightly to the right. We will descend using the path on the left but, for now, we need to galvanise ourselves for the steep, direct assault of the **path on the right**.

3 Head straight up and **slightly to the right**, through boggy ground. The path steepens and becomes a series of footsteps cut by generations of walkers. The staircase leads steadily upwards and steepens. At points if you stand straight and extend an arm you can touch the hillside in front of you. Even though you are breathing heavily keep an eye on your footwork as the ground is steep and often slippery. Just as the slope reaches maximum steepness at a small rocky gully we arrive at a terrace running around the upper hillside. Looking up and to the left we notice an exposure of weathered hexagonal basalt columns, a glimpse into Dumgoyne's volcanic core.

4 **Walk right** (south) for a few metres on the terrace. Although the terrace continues, we will leave it after just a few metres. A faint line of footsteps continues steeply up and **left** in a sort of gully. Go up here, stay in the footsteps and be careful as small stones here are like ball bearings under your boots! On the upper hill follow the obvious path over a fore-summit to reach the summit marker, a standing stone.

5 Take a well-earned rest and enjoy the views. With our backs to the summit, looking west, ahead are the Kilpatrick Hills. Another little volcanic plug, Duncolm, marks their highest point. Moving clockwise we can see the wide southern basin of Loch Lomond, spattered with islands, along the Highland Boundary Fault line. To the north-west are the Luss Hills; on a clear day the Arrochar Alps and The Cobbler are easily spotted. Further to the north lies Conic Hill, dwarfed by the backdrop of Ben Lomond. To the right (east) of Ben Lomond are the Trossachs: Ben Venue and then Ben Ledi. Looking east the views of the Campsie Fells and the Slackdhu escarpment are closer. In the distance to the south is the solitary pyramid of Tinto in the Southern Uplands. Back towards our starting point we look down the Clyde Valley with Glasgow sprawled out below. If it is an evening ascent the lights of the city will provide a spectacular finale to our summit panorama. To descend **head west**, back along the ascent path, but after 100 metres look for the faint path branching down **left** (south-west). Take this path downwards and **left** across some rocky slabs and then **turn gradually right** to the start of the terrace that we crossed on the way up. The path heads **north** along this terrace, initially above a steep crag, so take care here. This is a great little aerial walkway; it leads us past the point where we stepped on to the terrace on the way up. Do not go back down the ascent route; **keep going along the terrace**. Cross some tricky rocky steps and then the path leads to broad, grassy slopes. **Turn left** and go down easy slopes heading for the stiles marking the entrance to the upper field. **Cross the stiles** and retrace our steps back to the start. A lot of hill in such a short outing!

Notes: The route is steep so take care with children. Immediately east of the summit marker grassy slopes steepen above a crag; accidents have happened here so don't let children run around the summit and don't go exploring in this direction!

04 Dumgoyne

THE ARROCHAR ALPS FROM NEAR THE SUMMIT OF DOUNE HILL

05 Northern Luss Hills

18.4km/11.4 miles

A stunning circuit of the northern part of the Luss Hills, taking in Beinn Eich, Beinn Lochain, Doune Hill, Mid Hill and Beinn Dubh.

Luss » Glen Luss » Beinn Eich » Beinn Lochain » Doune Hill » Mid Hill » Beinn Dubh » Luss

Start
Luss car park (parking charge).
GR: NS 359931.

The Walk
Luss, on the bonnie banks of Loch Lomond, is the quintessential lochside village. Narrow streets, cottages, scones, tartan trinket shops, a beach and even TV fame have created, at peak times, a traffic-choked tourist trap. To the west of the village, across the A82, are the Luss Hills. Steep ridges and deep glens with fantastic potential for short outings, medium outings and downright hard days! Glen Luss divides these hills into a northern group, whose apex is Doune Hill (734 metres), and a southern range, culminating in Beinn Chaorach at 713 metres. In this walk we explore the northern hills in one big loop, with a sting in the middle rather than the tail!

As is often the case with lower hills the views here are surprisingly stunning. These are the highest tops at the southern end of Loch Lomond, and they mark the start of the Western Highlands. This walk is a long one, but it could be split and shortened at various stages. However, the entire circuit is worth the effort. Views on the first half are all about the Arrochar Alps and the Clyde seaboard. The second half is all about Loch Lomond and its islands. Best done in spring or autumn when the bracken is at its lowest, best on a clear day for the views and best take extra food and water as this is going to be a hard one.

NORTHERN LUSS HILLS
DISTANCE: 18.4KM/11.4 MILES » **TOTAL ASCENT**: 1,397M/4,583FT » **START GR**: NS 359931 » **TIME**: ALLOW 6–8 HOURS **SATNAV**: G83 8PA » **MAP**: OS EXPLORER OL39, LOCH LOMOND NORTH, 1:25,000 » **REFRESHMENTS**: MULTIPLE OUTLETS IN LUSS VILLAGE » **NAVIGATION**: MOSTLY ON GOOD PATHS; SOME ROUGH GROUND AND MAP NEEDED ON CENTRAL PATHLESS SECTION.

DAY WALKS IN LOCH LOMOND & THE TROSSACHS

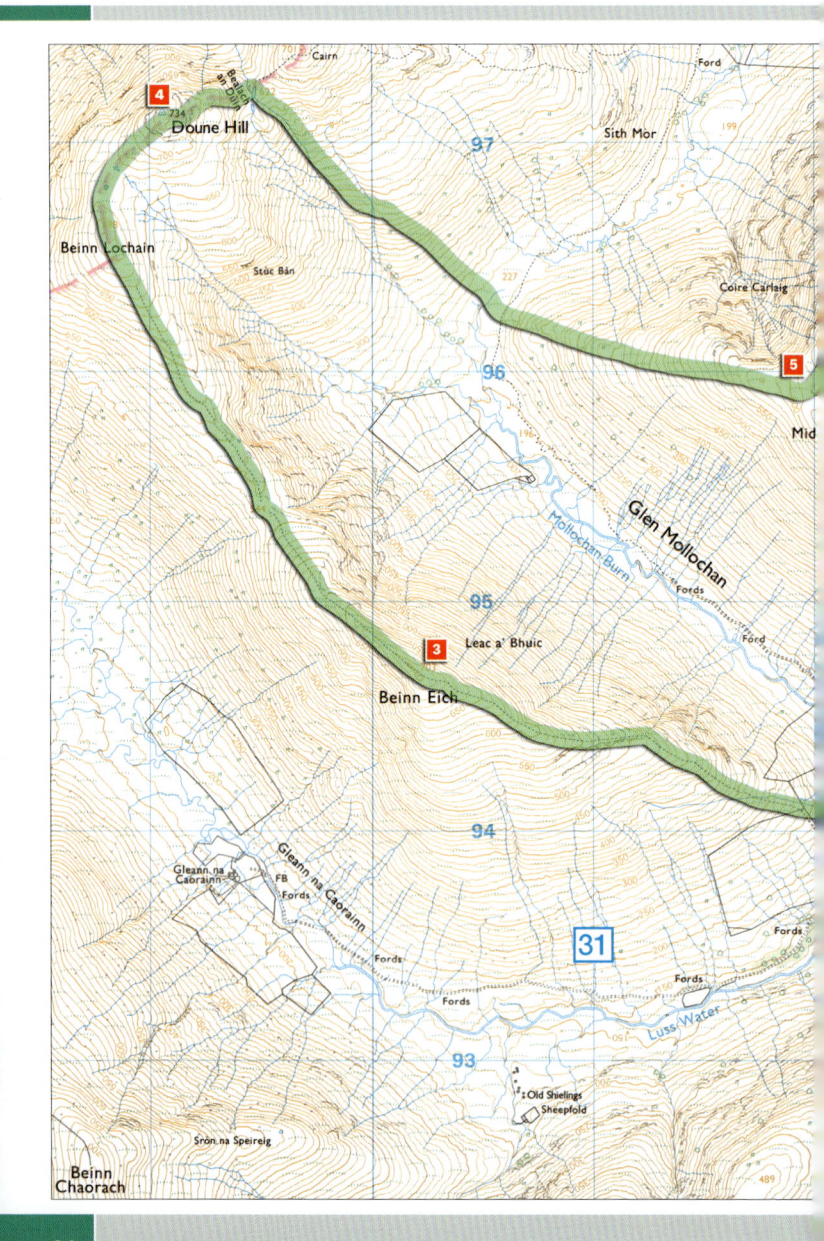

05 **Northern Luss Hills**

Directions – Northern Luss Hills

S➤ Walk **south** from the car park and **cross the A82** on an arched wooden bridge. At the western end of the bridge, **ignore** signs for *Beinn Dubh* (this is where we will finish). Go along the single-track road **north-west** into Glen Luss for 3.2km. **Ignore** roads going off to the left. Pass a turning area below the south-east ridge of Mid Hill (our second escape point) then follow the road **sharp left over a bridge** and continue round to the **right** on a farm road heading towards houses at Edentaggart. Before the buildings at the end of the straight section there is a stile and the remains of a signpost (NS 325941). This is where we get out on to the hillside.

2 **Cross the stile** and go up the track to Glen Mollochan. After 100m, go up and **left** towards a large ladder stile across a stone wall. Soon we can see that the stile is redundant as the wall has fallen down! Beyond the wall it is very muddy for a bit then we start steeply up the eastern ridge of Beinn Eich. **Pass to the left (south) of a small outcrop** then go steeply up the ridge. Eventually the angle eases and a path leads to the top. Beinn Eich has a low stone cairn. Take a rest here and enjoy the views, Ben More and Stob Binnein are easily spotted to the north and look misleadingly close.

3 Head **north-west** on a good path towards Beinn Lochain, a fore-summit of our target, Doune Hill. The walking is easy and views are starting to open up. Cross Beinn Lochain, then head **north** over a bealach and climb up grassy slopes to the summit of Doune Hill. The trig point calls for a detailed look at the 360-degree view. To the north we can see Beinn Narnain. Rotating clockwise we can see A'Chrois and, lower and closer, is Tullich Hill above Glen Douglas. To the north-east we can see the Crianlarich Hills, with Ben More and Stob Binnein prominent. Ben Lomond presents a broad side, revealing the length of its summit ridge. Rowardennan lies below on the shores of Loch Lomond. Then over the islands scattered through the southern basin of the loch. Looking south we can see the Leven Valley, then the Clyde Estuary, Arran and Dunoon. Cnoc Coinnich is to the west and then we swing past The Brack to The Cobbler and our starting position. It is worth lingering here to enjoy the vista and to fuel up for the next section.

4 Leave the summit heading **east**, towards the bealach at 622m. There is a lovely little lochan here, but no sign of a path. Take the easiest line, heading **east** down steep, rough and pathless hillside towards the floor of the glen 400m below. This is rough walking and the floor of the glen with its bogs and tussocks is even worse. Ahead of us to the east, a broad ridge forms the edge of a steep corrie, Coire Carlaig. We now have 400m of ascent on pathless, steep hillside to gain Mid Hill. (Escape is possible here to the south-east along Glen Mollochan back to the road just north of Edentaggart.) But let's finish the route. Take a deep breath and **start up the western ridge** of Mid Hill. Eventually the gradient eases. Head east along a broad ridge towards small cairns marking the top of Mid Hill. (An escape down the south-east ridge of Mid Hill leads easily to the turning area on the road below. However, there is little to be saved in distance or effort and by now the whole traverse is almost in the bag.)

5 From Mid Hill follow an easy path **north-east** over a minor top, then **east** then **south-east** towards the broad summit of Beinn Dubh. There are a few ups and downs but the path is much easier now. At one point (NS 327962) there is a spectacular view to the north down a steep-sided corrie to Glen Douglas and Inverbeg. On the summit of Beinn Dubh pause to look back towards the start of the route. We can feel smug that we didn't take the shortcuts! **Follow the path down the ridge towards Luss**, clearly visible below. The views to the loch are special and you might even see the seaplane pass below you. The path turns south through mixed woodland and then we are down, just a field to cross before the footbridge, and then back to the car park. With luck we will be in time for tea and cake or something a little stronger!

Notes: This route is long with rough terrain so give yourself plenty of time. The shortcuts may reduce the effort but once down on the tarmac road you would almost certainly regret not having completed the full route.

LOOKING BACK TO BEINN EICH FROM THE SLOPES OF BEINN LOCHAIN

Section 2

The Trossachs

Lying to the east of Loch Lomond the scenic, rolling land of the Trossachs makes great walking country, amid heather-clad hills, sparkling waterfalls and myriad lochs. While lacking the height of the northern hills, the rocky and undulating character of these hills provide strenuous and rugged outings amid stunning scenery.

WATERFALLS NEAR BEN VENUE (ROUTE 6)

THE VIEW NORTH FROM BEN VENUE (ROUTE 6)

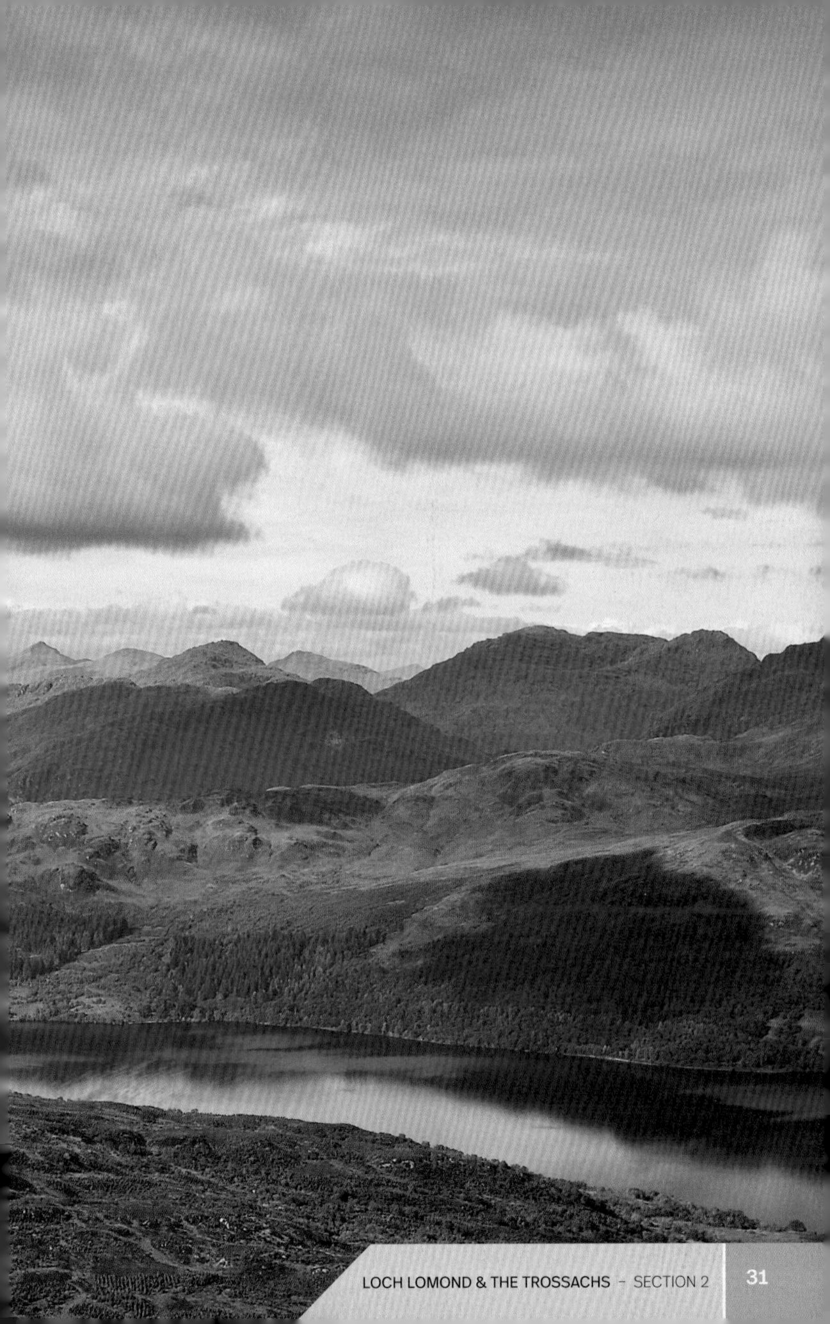

BEN VENUE REFLECTED IN LOCH ACHRAY

06 Ben Venue

13.3km/8.3 miles

The wee mountain, at the very heart of the Trossachs.

Loch Achray » Gleann Riabhach » Bealach with large carin » Summits (east and west) » Bealach with large cairn » Gleann Riabhach » Loch Achray

Start
Ben Venue car park (parking charge), western end of Loch Achray.
GR: NN 506069.

The Walk
There is a story, probably untrue, that the first European to arrive in Australia asked a native Australian what that strange, hopping animal was called? The local replied 'kangaroo'. The story goes that 'kangaroo' is Aboriginal for 'I don't know'! Something similar might well have happened when the first English 'explorer' arrived in the wild Trossachs. Pointing upwards our proto-tourist said 'I say fine fellow, what is that mountain called'? 'A'Bheinn Mheanbh' (pronounced 'Ben Venav') was the Gael's reply, and so Ben Venue was deemed close enough and on to the maps it went.

A'Bheinn Mheanbh means the 'wee mountain' – a strange title for the hill that dominates the central Trossachs. Only from the south can we see Ben Venue as the little sibling of Ben Lomond to the west and Ben Ledi to the east.

The walk starts as a lovely forest walk, on boardwalks and good, waymarked paths. We cross waterfalls and wind through resinous pines with all the sounds and smells of the forest, ideally on a crisp autumn or spring morning. Higher up, the path contours through felled forestry. Take a good look at what is left behind after the forest has been harvested, it is the only terrain that can stop even the complete mountaineer, or a kangaroo for that matter. Maps don't accurately show the coming and going of plantations, so it is best to stick to paths and not to go exploring, believe me! On the summit ridge there is a feast of mountains for us to name and a new challenge too: name that loch. So, kangaroo, Ben Venue, whatever, let's enjoy our outing on this big, wee mountain.

BEN VENUE

DISTANCE: 13.3KM/8.3 MILES » **TOTAL ASCENT**: 666M/2,185FT » **START GR**: NN 506069 » **TIME**: ALLOW 5-6 HOURS
SATNAV: FK17 8HZ » **MAP**: OS EXPLORER OL46, THE TROSSACHS, 1:25,000 » **REFRESHMENTS**: NUMEROUS OUTLETS IN NEARBY ABERFOYLE OR CALLANDER » **NAVIGATION**: STRAIGHTFORWARD; GOOD PATHS ALL THE WAY.

VIEW FROM THE SUMMIT OF BEN VENUE

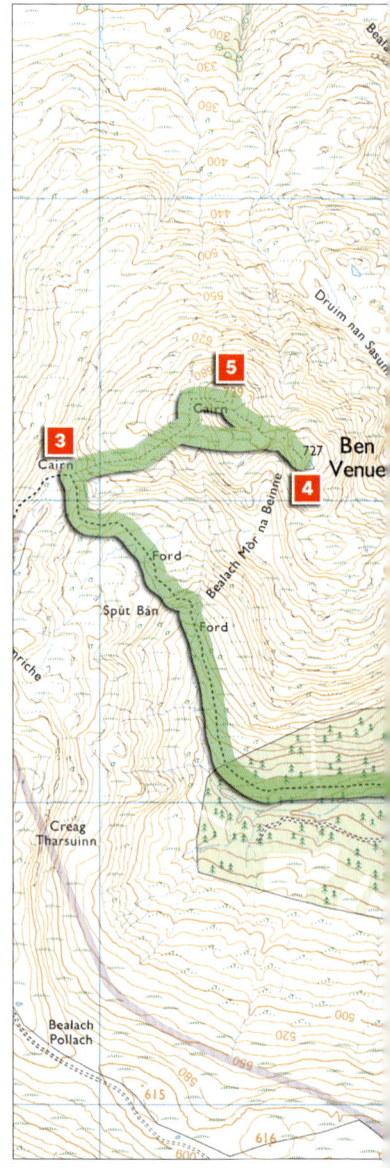

DAY WALKS IN LOCH LOMOND & THE TROSSACHS

Loch Lomond and Trossachs National Park

06 Ben Venue

Directions – Ben Venue

S> From the south-west corner of the car park a **broad path winds up through the woodland**. *Ben Venue Hill Path* is signposted at every junction; just follow the signs. Walk parallel to the Pass of Trossachs road, with views north to Ben A'an rising above the forest. After a lay-by, **turn left** through iron gates and walk up a tarmac road signposted *Loch Katrine Dam*. In Achray Water on our left we can often spot dippers. After 300m take a path down and **left to a bridge** over some waterfalls. After the bridge, **turn right** on to a wide forest track, then after 300m **turn left**. At a junction with a forestry road **turn left** and after 100m **turn right**, heading uphill through the trees. At another forestry road a signpost warns us that the waymarking ends and reminds us to be suitably equipped for the hill. **Cross the forestry road diagonally and start up the hill path heading west.**

2 Waymarks have stopped but the path is wide and obvious all the way to the summit. This long section winds around the southern flank of Ben Venue through felled forest. Climb steadily up and round to the **right** (north-west) with open views and a waterfall to take our minds off the effort. We now reach the only section of poor path on the entire route. The path crosses a wide swamp; aim for a white marker post in the middle (perhaps it had a lifebelt once) to avoid the deepest bits of the bog. Once safely across, head up over some steep slabs using our hands for balance. Head **north-west** and arrive at an outrageously big cairn on the bealach.

3 We are now on the summit ridge and the views are already eye-poppingly good! Go up and round to the **right** (north-east) on steep terrain, using our hands for balance. Numerous ups and downs and rocky sections lead to a final steep climb and a summit with a stone trig point. This top of Ben Venue is 727m and is not the true summit! The true summit is 2m higher and 360m to the north-west; we will go there on the way down. Stand beside the trig point and enjoy the view. To the north we can see the Crianlarich Munros across the trench of Loch Katrine. Moving clockwise, we see Ben More, then Ben Vorlich and Stùc a'Chroin. Continuing round, we look down to Loch Achray and Loch Venachar and, south-east of these, is the little Loch Drunkie. To the south lies the Blane Valley with the northern escarpment of the Campsie Fells and Dumgoyne. Continuing clockwise we can see the Kilpatrick Hills and, on clear days, Arran, before the foreground is filled by Ben Lomond. To the west the Arrochar Alps fill the horizon (can we name them all?). Returning to our starting point we look across Loch Arklet to Cruach Ardrain and Beinn Tulaichean. Now let's visit the true summit on our way down.

4 Below the summit block a faint path heads off **right**. This path winds over and around some outcrops and leads to a cairn marking the true summit at 729m. The views here are dominated by the uninterrupted sweep of Loch Katrine.

5 From the true summit **retrace your steps to the main path** or, in good visibility, take a direct line south, carefully, down some steep ground to the main path. At the big cairn on the bealach turn **left**. Once back in the forest follow signs back to the starting point. There are cafes and bars in Aberfoyle, Loch Katrine and Callander. For those of a more energetic persuasion, there is a choice of lochs for a refreshing swim.

Notes: An alternative ascent can be made from the south above Ledard Farm on the shores of Loch Ard. This also needs an out-and-back approach and involves a tricky river crossing. Any descent to the west is complicated by forestry and routes via Bealach nam Bo to the north involve extremely rough terrain. In summary, there is no easy circular route of Ben Venue.

UPPER PATH ON BEN VENUE

ON THE DESCENT TOWARDS LOCH LUBNAIG

07 Ben Ledi

9.9km/6.2 miles

A leisurely circuit of this very popular mountain.

Car park near metal bridge » Garbh Uisge » Stank Glen » Bealach nan Corp » Ben Ledi » A'Chioch » Car park near metal bridge

Start
Small car park at the southern end of Loch Lubnaig (cross a metal bridge from the A84 to reach it).
GR: NN 587091.

The Walk
Ben Ledi stands all alone, dominating the skyline north of Callander. Viewed from the south-east, its long, gentle profile and flattish summit explains the name: 'the hill of the long slope'. Its isolation, above the flatlands to the south, affords wide summit views and its proximity to Stirling and Callander make 'Ledi' one of our busiest hills.

Our route is a circular one, up the unpleasant sounding Stank Glen. Stank means drain or gutter and, for years, this route was a notorious bog. It is now much less of a 'stank' thanks to a new path. The path climbs on to the northern ridge of Ben Ledi at the Bealach nan Corp, south of the small Lochan nan Corp. 'Nan Corp' means of the corpse or body. This was once a coffin route; like sombre drove roads, these were routes to carry the deceased over the mountains to clan burial grounds on the other side. Legend has it that a burial party was crossing, from Glen Finglas to St Brides Chapel at the southern end of Loch Lubnaig, when a winter storm rolled in. In the white-out, the procession walked on to the frozen surface of Lochan nan Corp, the ice broke and down went the coffin and the pall bearers; all were lost. Bad luck indeed, especially as it is really quite a small lochan!

The trig point of Ben Ledi is upstaged by a nearby iron cross memorial. Iron crosses are unusual here but are a common sight in the Alps. This memorial is to a mountain rescuer who sadly lost his life during a rescue on Ben More. Whatever your views on memorials, this cross is a striking visual presence and, while walking a compass bearing in a white-out, I have been glad to see it appear, rimed in ice!

BEN LEDI
DISTANCE: 9.9KM/6.2 MILES » **TOTAL ASCENT**: 766M/2,513FT » **START GR**: NN 587091 » **TIME**: ALLOW 5 HOURS
SATNAV: FK17 8HF » **MAP**: OS EXPLORER OL46, THE TROSSACHS, 1:25,000 » **REFRESHMENTS**: NUMEROUS OPTIONS IN CALLANDER » **NAVIGATION**: GOOD PATH ALL THE WAY.

Directions – Ben Ledi

S Walk **north**, back towards the metal bridge. Ignore signposts for *Ben Ledi* on the left; we will come down this way. **Follow the road** north with the Garbh Uisge on our right for 1.2km. Just before the first buildings take a path off to the **left** through a gap in the barrier. This path joins the broad forestry road (blue marker post). In about 250m the track bends left, but we take the narrow path heading **right**, into the woods at the apex of the bend. This narrow path turns to the left, climbs alongside a burn and heads to the west up Stank Glen. This cuts out the zigzags of the forestry road. Cross the road again and regain our path. There is an impressive waterfall down to our right.

2 After crossing the road again, marker posts and a barrier signal the start of the open hillside. Follow the path through newly planted birch trees past a small hydro scheme. Views are opening out and the walking is easy. We are following the Stank Glen Loop Walk. Just before the path loops back on itself look for a narrow path heading off to the **left** (west); this is our climb up to Bealach nan Corp.

3 Climb steeply towards Bealach nan Corp. Behind us are excellent views towards Stirling, the National Wallace Monument and the Ochil Hills. The path leads to the 'pass of the corpse' which, despite its name, is a lovely viewpoint. (To see the lethal lochan, walk to the right.) Once we have soaked up the views, head **south** on the obvious path towards the pointed fore-summit above. Once we crest the ridge, we can see the summit trig point. Climb around the rim of the wonderfully steep north-east corrie and then suddenly we are at the summit of Ben Ledi. Let's look in detail at the view. Looking north, we can see the Crianlarich Munros with Ben More and Stob Binnein. Moving clockwise, we have Meall nan Tarmachan, then Beinn Each, the low hills above Callander, and then the Kippen Flats with the Touch Hills beyond. To the south we can see the pointed Meikle Bin, then, further south-west, Dumgoyne. Continuing clockwise we see the curiously named Loch Drunkie, then Glen Finglas Reservoir with Ben Venue behind it. Ben Lomond and the northern end of Loch Katrine complete the circuit. Around the summit there are various rocks that offer shelter for our lunch but take care to avoid the deposits of human ashes!

4 Leave the summit heading **south-east** on a broad path. The descent steepens and becomes quite rocky before turning to the **left** (heading north) across the side of the ridge. The path leads down through partially felled forest. The views to the north along Loch Lubnaig are special. The trail crosses a forestry road at a signpost to the

Car Park. Pass a war memorial and soon we are at the finishing line, near the bridge. **Turn right** and head back to the car park.

Notes: This route could be done in either direction, but the views are superior this way and it is likely to be much less busy on the ascent. An out-and-back via the normal route (our descent) would be quicker. Go early as the car park is notoriously busy.

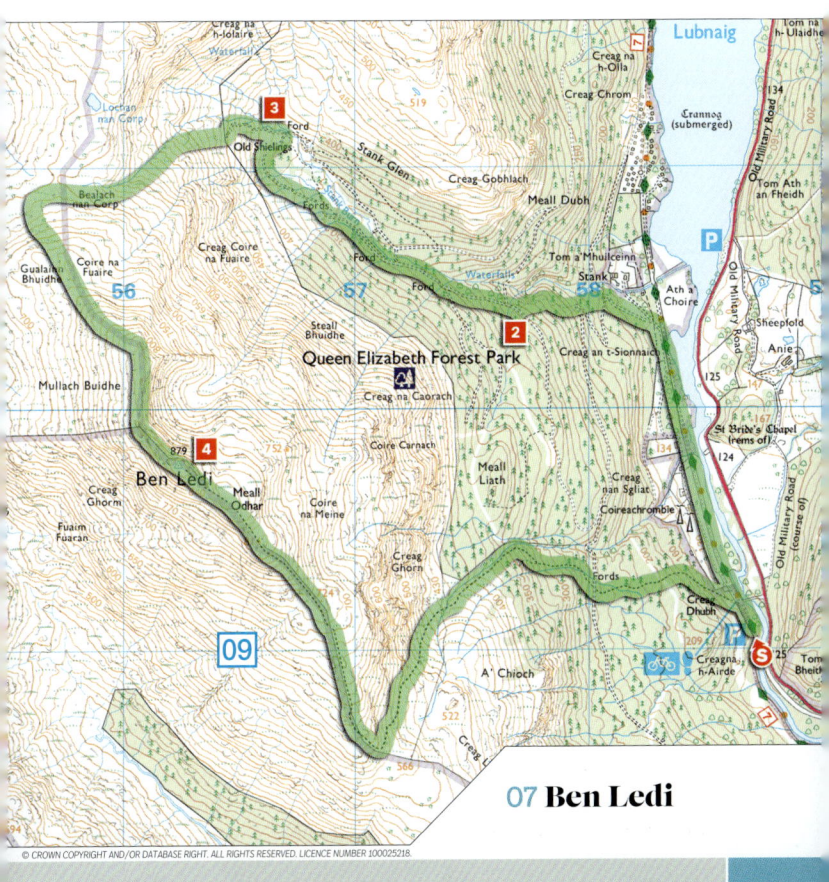

07 Ben Ledi

HEADING TOWARDS BEN A'AN

08 Ben A'an

3.8km/2.4 miles

A pleasant, short outing to the Trossachs' most popular pocket mountain.

Loch Achray » Forest » Steep ascent » Ben A'an » Steep descent » Forest » Loch Achray

Start
Ben A'an car park (parking charge), north of Loch Achray. GR: NN 509070. Additional parking available at Ben Venue car park (parking charge; GR: NN 506069), 500m to the west along the A821.

The Walk
When we think of a perfect mountain, we imagine it rising from a forest to a rocky pyramid with steep cliffs and a perfect pointed summit spire, the top just big enough for one person to stand on. Ben A'an is pretty to close to that ideal, but it is a scaled-down version, and, in truth, it is a bit of a fraud. The peak is in fact only a spur on the southern flank of a sprawling, lumpy, heather-clad hill, but its outline, its splendid summit and views allow us to forget those shortcomings. Once on top we can scramble up to the very pointed rocky summit. Sitting on top looking to the north-west, it is easy to see how the rough, heathery hills and deep lochs of *Rob Roy* country inspired Sir Walter Scott's romantic writings. Below us lies deep Loch Katrine, the main water supply for Glasgow. The water is carried by two 41-kilometre aqueducts that gravity-feed water to reservoirs at Milngavie, north of Glasgow. The water-works were so special that they were opened by Queen Victoria herself in 1859. Today, a steamship named after Sir Walter Scott runs on Loch Katrine.

Heather-clad hills, *Rob Roy*, Queen Victoria, Sir Walter Scott – it is all very Scottish, kitsch and romantic. Even the engines of the little steamship are powered by biofuels, so that the good citizens of Glasgow don't get a very un-romantic taste of diesel in their drinking water.

BEN A'AN

DISTANCE: 3.8KM/2.4 MILES » **TOTAL ASCENT**: 366M/1,201FT » **START GR**: NN 509070 » **TIME**: ALLOW 3 HOURS
SATNAV: FK17 8HY » **MAP**: OS EXPLORER OL46, THE TROSSACHS, 1:25,000 » **REFRESHMENTS**: NUMEROUS OUTLETS IN ABERFOYLE OR CALLANDER » **NAVIGATION**: STRAIGHTFORWARD; WIDE, OBVIOUS PATH.

Directions – Ben A'an

S From the car park, cross the road then follow a signpost marking the start of the broad path leading up through recently thinned out woodland. After 100m **ignore** a path going off to the left and continue **straight ahead**. The path steepens and climbs up and round to the **left** on big stone steps before curving **right** at a small bridge over a lovely burn. **Cross the bridge** and follow the path up to a more level section, before climbing again and crossing small burns on large stepping stones.

2 The summit pyramid is now visible straight ahead. Continue **straight ahead** (north-west) through woodland of birch and rowan to a flat open area on the left. This marks the start of the steep final climb. There are big flat boulders here with curious linear furrows. Given what lies ahead, it might be an idea to stop here for a breather and a drink.

3 Head steeply up on big stone blocks. If you are doing this properly you will be breathing heavily by now! Cross some steep, eroded rocks and a small burn. Hands are needed but only for balance and before long the path levels off. Cross a bog on big stepping stones then go up a steep, rocky section to the small summit area. The true summit is obvious and is one of the most photogenic spots in Scotland. Scramble to the top taking great care on the highly polished slabs. Like our ideal mountain there is only room for one or two people on top. Be aware that the slopes in front of the summit area (to the south and west) lead steeply to the crags below.

LOCH KATRINE FROM THE SUMMIT OF BEN A'AN

4 Time for the 360-degree views. Ben Venue is just to the south-west across Loch Katrine. From Ben Venue rotate clockwise to the north-west and spot the unmistakeable outline of The Cobbler then the flat top of Beinn Narnain, then round to A'Chrois, Beinn Ime, Ben Vane and Ben Vorlich. Further to the north we see Stob a'Choin and Beinn Tulaichean. As we turn further around it all goes a bit pear-shaped as we realise that we are only on a low summit on the side of the rather un-special Meall Gainmheich. Alright, so let's skip a few and look south over Loch Achray. In the distance we can see Dumgoyne, then across the Blane Valley to the Kilpatrick Hills and back to our start point, Ben Venue. To descend we simply a **reverse our route**. As we wind down the lower section of the path the impressive spires of the Tigh Mor (Big House) remind us of the Victorian heritage of this area. Mind you, Big House (or Big Hoose) has different connotations for the Glaswegians who take the waters … so to speak.

Notes: This is a very popular walk. It is steeper than you think. Leave early if you want to get parked and stay late if you want a splendid sunset from the summit.

08 Ben A'an

Section 3

Arrochar Alps

Affectionately and accurately referred to as the Arrochar Alps, this compact group of rugged mountains offers the walker a chance to explore steeper and more challenging terrain. Forming an arc around the northern end of Loch Lomond and Loch Long above the village of Arrochar, these hills are famous among rock climbers and provide stunning views into the fjord land of Argyll. The iconic Cobbler is the most striking 'trophy summit' of the group.

STEEP DESCENT FROM BEN VANE (ROUTE 15)

LOCHAN BELOW THE SUMMIT RIDGE OF THE BRACK (ROUTE 14)

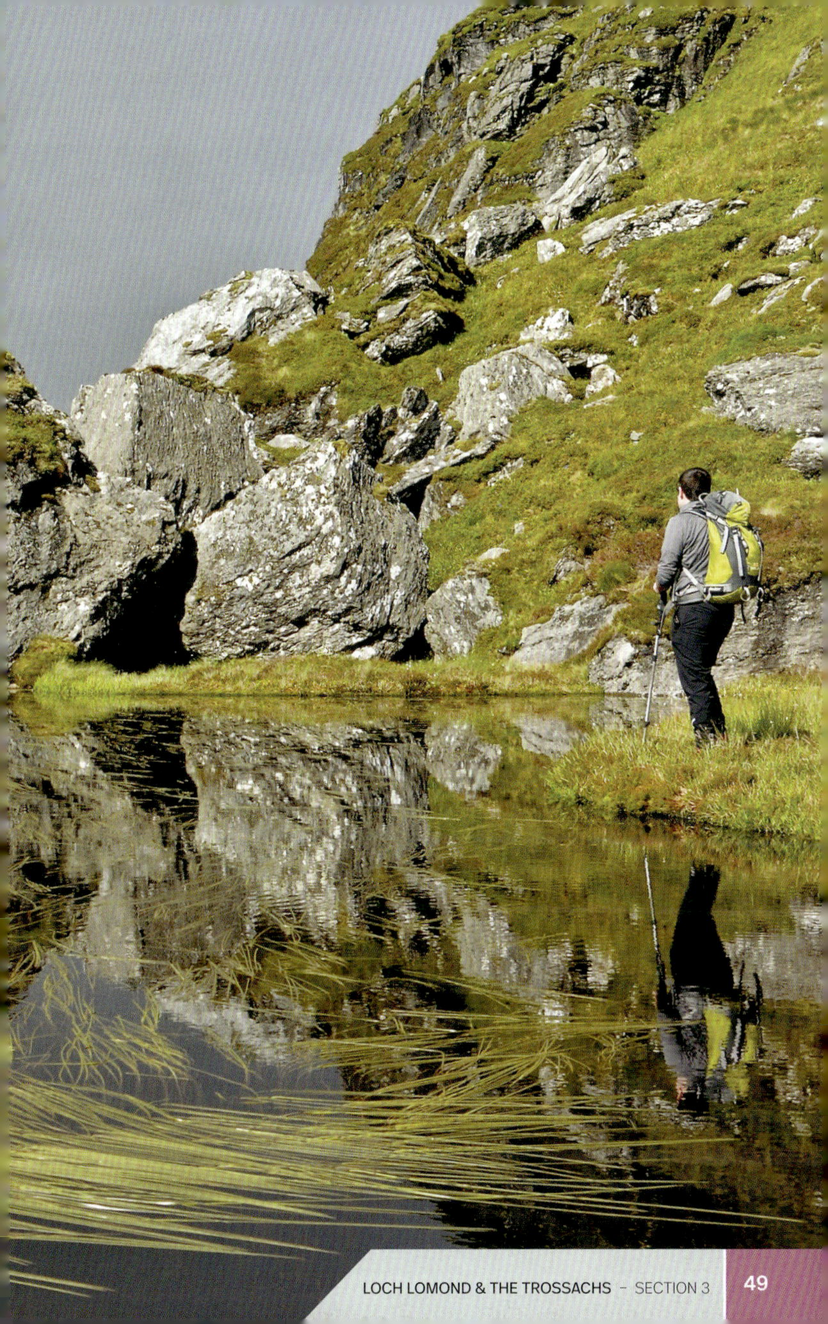

LOOKING TOWARDS LOCH SLOY FROM CRUACH TAIRBEIRT

09 Cruach Tairbeirt

4.1km/2.5 miles

A test of endurance as we navigate the forest to reach a visual sweet spot above the lochs.

Arrochar & Tarbet station » Cruach Tairbeirt » Arrochar and Tarbet Link Path » Arrochar & Tarbet station

Start
**Arrochar & Tarbet station.
GR: NN 311045. Limited parking at the station. Either arrive by train or park in nearby Tarbet or Arrochar.**

The Walk
Cruach Tairbeirt, the 'stack of the boat drag', doesn't sound much but, don't be fooled, this is a wee cracker of a hill! Driving north along the A82 approaching the village of Tarbet, our hill sits squat in front of A'Chrois. Houses are dotted here and there on its lower slopes which are clad in the natural mixed woodland of the Argyll Forest. Higher up, Cruach Tairbeirt has been heavily planted with dense conifer forests. If the density of the forest itself was not enough to severely impede access, then the clearing of the forests now taking place has certainly added another layer of challenge. This hill is worth the challenge and on a clear day the views from its unique central position are astounding.

'Boat drag' refers to a *tarbet* (more often *tarbert*), a narrow strip of land between bodies of water over which boats can be portaged. In 1263 Vikings sailed up Loch Long, dragged their boats from Arrochar across the glen to Tarbet from where they put in again. Once on Loch Lomond, they set about doing very Viking things, mainly raiding and pillaging. Genetic studies of the local MacFarlane Clan suggest they did a bit of the other too. Like most tourists the Vikings visited Luss; a burial stone can be seen there to this day.

This hill lends itself to circular routes; however, forest clearing operations have left us with only one reliable route, an out-and-back. The industrial scale of the forest clearing means that exploration of the hillside is impossible due to mud and broken branches that could stop a panzer division. Don't go when the bracken is at its highest; pick a cold autumn day or a crisp spring morning, perhaps when the big hills have snow on top. Sublime.

CRUACH TAIRBEIRT
DISTANCE: 4.1KM/2.5 MILES » **TOTAL ASCENT**: 373M/1,224FT » **START GR**: NN 311045 » **TIME**: ALLOW 3 HOURS
SATNAV: G83 7DA » **MAP**: OS EXPLORER OL39, LOCH LOMOND NORTH, 1:25,000 » **REFRESHMENTS**: TARBET TEAROOM OR THE SLANJ, TARBET » **NAVIGATION**: TRICKY DUE TO FORESTRY WORKS BUT PATH STILL INTACT.

Directions – Cruach Tairbeirt

S Go through the station underpass, **turn sharp left** and head up the path into the woodland of oak, beech and birch. At a signpost and wooden barrier, a notice says the walk is no longer promoted by the Forestry Commission. This refers to the Cruach Tairbeirt Loop Walk, not our ascent. **Turn right** past the barrier and follow the broad path up and round to the **left**. Pass a concrete structure in the burn on our right and continue up. We arrive at an ugly, newly cut, logging road. Go **straight across** the road to the path climbing steeply up ahead. Follow this steep path until it starts to bend to the right (north-east). **Ignore** a path going off to the left and **cross the small burn**. After crossing the burn, we are in an area of brash, tree stumps and branches where the forest has been cleared. Twenty or so paces after the burn look out for a new path that is starting to form through this brash on the **left**. Follow this subtle path over the broken branches. Head north, up towards the remaining tall trees ahead of us.

2 Enter the forest at a wide avenue through very tall trees. Look back to see Ben Lomond rising above the loch. Go up through the forest; it is very atmospheric and helpful locals have tied markers to the trees to guide us. After 200m **turn right** (this turning is marked by a tag on a tree and a small painted boulder; at the time of writing the boulder was painted to look like a sort of sad fish!); this leads us over muddy and boggy ground out of the trees. Take care around a fallen tree and then head out on to the open hillside. The path winds through bracken (hopefully brown and withered) and up to a small crag. Go steeply up around the crag of folded schist then **curve to the right**, cross a flat area then go steeply up beside a small outcrop. Hands help with balance here. Head straight up towards a solitary small conifer then **turn right** on boggy ups and downs towards the summit of Cruach Tairbeirt.

3 The trig point has been recently painted. The view is superb with mountains, glens and lochs all around. To the north is Ben Vorlich, rising above the Sloy Dam. Moving clockwise there is Beinn Chabhair then Beinn Tulaichean. Inversnaid lies below in the east with Ben Lomond towering above the loch. To the south is Beinn Bhreac and Ben Reoch. Now we look across Loch Long to The Brack, The Cobbler and Beinn Narnain. Continuing clockwise we have the south face of A'Chrois with the slot of Chrois Gully below the summit. On past Ben Vane to Loch Sloy to complete the revolution. Once we have had our fill of the summit views, walk south for 60m on a faint path to a rocky edge and look straight down to the loch and Tarbet far below.

Go back to the trig point. The descent **follows the outward route**; take great care to stick to the path. Enter the forest at the sloping ramp through the trees and go back down to the forestry road.

4 At the forest road we can cross over and go back down the way we came up. But for variety **turn right** and walk along the forest road for about 400m. At a marker post **turn left** (south-east) into the lower woodland. Now head back on this section of the Arrochar and Tarbet Link Path. After a steep uphill section, we are back at the signpost where we set off earlier. **Turn right** and go down to the underpass. There are cafes and pubs nearby in both Tarbet and in Arrochar, or swimming can be enjoyed in the bay at Tarbet!

Notes: This route may disappear with forest clearing work, however I think it will survive for some time yet. The plan for Cruach Tairbeirt is for the forest to be cleared and the natural woodland restored. At all times, obey all signs and keep away from areas of active forestry!

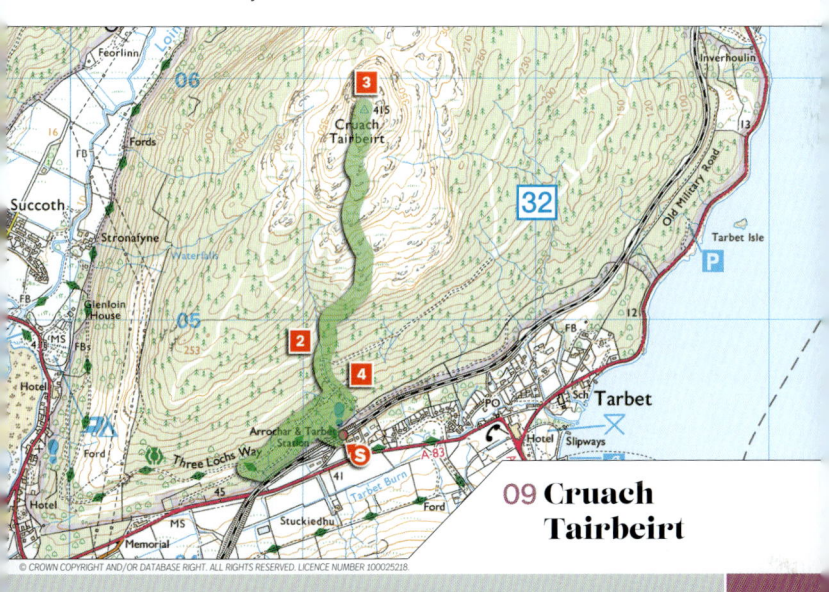

09 Cruach Tairbeirt

LOOKING SOUTH-WEST FROM THE SUMMIT OF NORTH PEAK

10 The Cobbler

10.9km/6.8 miles

The most iconic mountain of the Arrochar Alps.

Arrochar » NN 268059 » The Cobbler » Bealach a'Mhaim » Arrochar

Start
Succoth car park, north of Arrochar (parking charge). GR: NN 295049. (Additional parking available at Loch Long car park (parking charge), 250m to the east on the A83. GR: NN 298049.)

The Walk
Before we start, let's be clear: this is The Cobbler. Seriously, no one who knows this famous mountain uses its Arthurian name. This triple-summited peak is the poster-boy of the area. Like those other Scottish icons – Buachaille Etive Mòr, Stac Pollaidh and Suilven – you never forget your first sight of The Cobbler. Viewed from Arrochar the summit thrusts three rocky peaks skywards creating an outline like no other mountain in the region. On the right, the North Peak crazily overhangs the main ridge. To the left, the South Peak (Arthur's Seat on the OS map) presents an alpine spire, a sort of *Arrocharhorn*! The little rocky peak in the centre, the least dramatic, is the summit of The Cobbler.

The highest point of the mountain is the pinnacle of The Cobbler. Standing right on the top requires a short, but serious climb on polished, smooth schist. Unless you have climbing experience, it is not recommended. Traversing a broad ledge on the left of the summit block leads to a hole in the summit, Argyll's Eye. Crawling through this is known as 'threading the needle' and it leads to a sloping ledge with a big drop below. This ledge is traversed until a short climb leads to the very top of the block. Reversing this on polished, slippery, outward-sloping rock is not easy and any slip would likely be fatal. Experienced climbers treat this with respect and never go near it in the wet.

The summit of the South Peak is the domain of rock climbers and there is no easy walking route. The North Peak can be accessed by a path. It is an exposed top with sloping slabs and big drops all around so, again, one for dry conditions.

Safely down in Arrochar, stop for some refreshment and look up to where you have just been. If someone asks you if you have just climbed Ben Arthur ... well, you know what to tell them!

THE COBBLER
DISTANCE: 10.9KM/6.8 MILES » **TOTAL ASCENT**: 870M/2,854FT » **START GR**: NN 295049 » **TIME**: ALLOW 5 HOURS
SATNAV: G83 7AP » **MAP**: OS EXPLORER OL39, LOCH LOMOND NORTH, 1:25,000 » **REFRESHMENTS**: ARROCHAR CHIPPY, BEN ARTHURS BOTHY OR THE VILLAGE INN, ARROCHAR » **NAVIGATION**: GOOD PATH ALL OF THE WAY. SOME EASY SCRAMBLING ON ASCENT (SEE NOTES ON TRUE SUMMIT).

Directions – The Cobbler

S The path starts opposite Succoth car park. **Follow the zigzags** through the forest to a bench beside a forestry road. **Turn left** towards an antenna. Before the antenna **turn right** on to a signposted path, heading uphill. This path meanders up through the forest with occasional views south-east towards Ben Lomond. The path feels quite enclosed, but soon heads steeply up and round to the **left** to leave the forest. Here we get our first view of today's target – a great spot for photographs.

2 Follow the path **north-west** with lots of ups and downs. The path winds around the Narnain Boulders. Under the biggest of these are the remains of a small wall built into this historic *howff*. A steep section of steps leads to a fork in the path. The fork is marked with a post bearing the grid reference: NN 268059.

3 **Turn left** at the post. **Cross a stream** on big stepping stones and head around to the **right**, where things start steepening up. The path is loose here, so take care. Hands help with balance. Scramble up a steep gully and top out on to a level section. Go up and to the **right**. We are getting closer to the buttresses of the North Peak above us, where we might spot some climbers. An awkward, short scramble leads to a section with tremendous views to the South Peak to our left. Keep to the path and boulder-hop steadily upwards to the bealach between the North Peak (on our right) and easy slopes leading to The Cobbler (on our left). Go up and **left** to the summit area beside the pinnacle of the true summit of The Cobbler. There is no trig point but let's take in the view anyway. To the south-east we can see Ben Lomond; moving clockwise we look over Ben Reoch, Tullich Hill and the Luss Hills then south-west down Loch Long. The South Peak partly blocks the distant views as we continue round. We can see The Brack, Ben Donich, Beinn an Lochain, Binnein an Fhìdhleir and then to the north Beinn Luibhean, Beinn Ime and Ben Vane come into view. Looking north-east we turn past Beinn Narnain back to our starting point of Ben Lomond. Mindful of the serious nature of the true summit we may be content with the fore-summit, anyway the views are not improved by the extra 8 metres!

4 Head back to the bealach*. At the bealach face north, follow the broad path to our **right**, descending gently in the direction of Beinn Ime. Follow the path; at a broad shoulder (NN 260063) it heads steeply down to the **right**. The path is steep but has big stone steps. Continue on until the main path just below the Bealach a'Mhaim (NN 261065).

10 The Cobbler

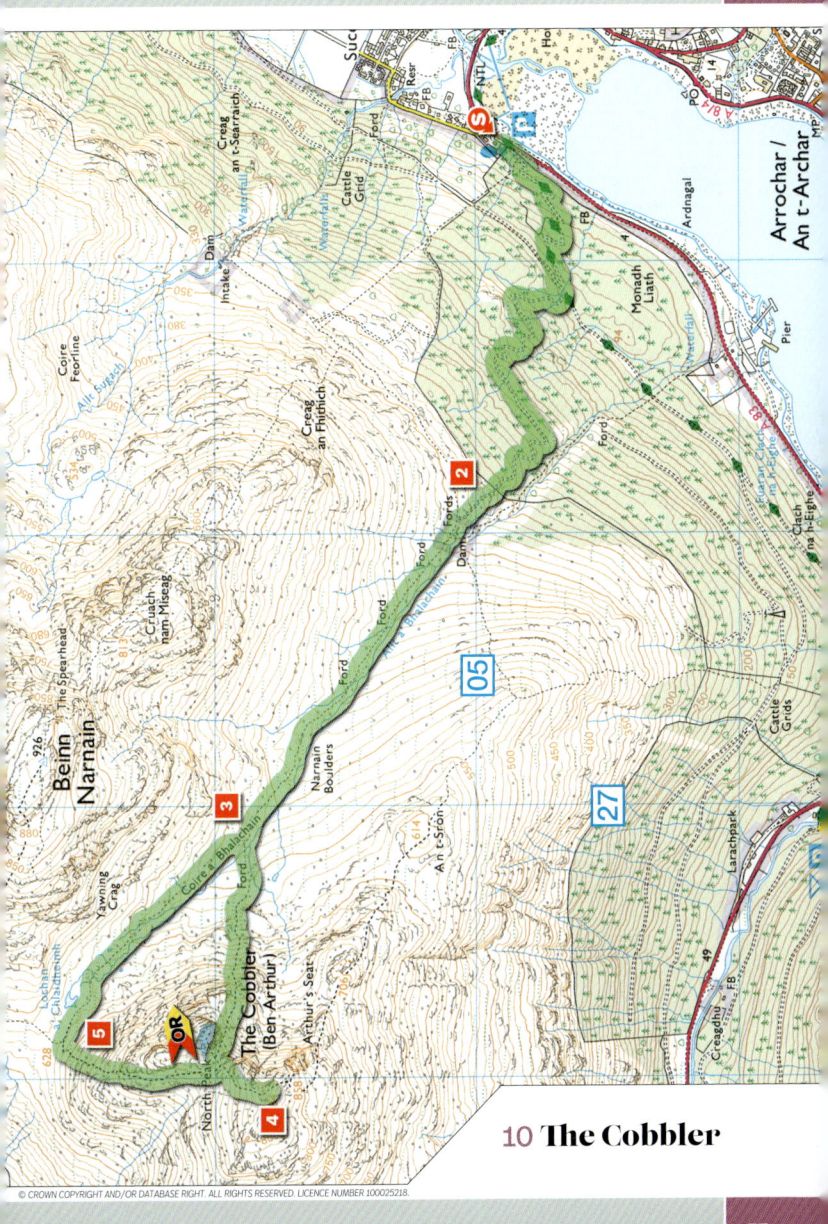

Directions – The Cobbler continued …

> **OR** *To visit the North Peak summit, from the bealach climb up and **left** on a narrow path. At easy-angled smooth slabs we have a choice. To our **left** a narrow path winds around a crag before turning **right** and going steeply up around some short walls. This leads to the North Peak summit block at its eastern edge. **Alternatively**, a faint path crosses the slabs before winding **left** along the edge of a steep drop and zigzagging to the summit. The top is a sloping slab surrounded by steep drops and marked with a cairn. Exposed and rocky, it is not a place for children to wander about and is best kept for a dry, windless day. To descend, **retrace our steps** back to the bealach before joining the descent path.

5 Turn **right** and follow the broad, easy path (heading south-east) to re-join our ascent path at the marker post (NN 268059). Now we simply retrace our steps back down to Arrochar and a well-earned celebratory refreshment. Looking upwards and trying to make the weird shapes of the summit rocks look like a shoemaker becomes easier the more we celebrate!

THE DESCENT PATH WITH BEINN IME STRAIGHT AHEAD

THE SUMMIT OF THE COBBLER

LOCH RESTIL

11 Beinn an Lochain

4.7km/2.9 miles

A steep, airy scramble to the summit of this former Munro.

A83 lay-by » North-east ridge » Beinn an Lochain » North-east ridge » A83 lay-by

Start
Lay-by on the western side of the A83, 1.7km north of Rest and be Thankful. GR: NN 234088.

The Walk
We like lists. Shopping lists; bucket lists; Munros; Corbetts; Seven Summits; 4,000-metre peaks – a sort of mountain trainspotting or Top Trumps. Lists exist to be ticked and completed. Sir Hugh Munro made a list of 3,000-foot (914-metre) mountains, and it included Beinn an Lochain. Subsequent surveys showed that the summit falls short of the magic height by 13 metres, and so it was deleted from this most revered of lists. Not a Munro: not interested? There are those who only stick to the list and miss out all the great hills that don't make the grade. Beinn an Lochain is a wasted day for the obsessed Munro-bagger, but ... what a way to waste a day.

I have wasted countless days on this lovely former Munro. Summer mornings, when I have crested the ridge and come eye to eye with a soaring eagle. Icy, winter days, where axe and crampon have been put to full use to achieve the summit. Stormy days, when I have opted for a longer but safer descent to avoid the *mauvais pas* above the crags.

The hill can be climbed quickly via the steep and direct north-east ridge. There are various places where hands are needed for balance and a bit more. It is steep, direct and often narrow. On one section any deviation from the path could put us on very dangerous ground. In winter this is a serious route. Failure to find a key part of the path in descent has led to numerous accidents; in poor visibility descend by safer slopes to the south using our optional route and walk back to the start. Once you have bagged this ex-Munro I am sure it will make it on to your list of favourite short outings.

BEINN AN LOCHAIN

DISTANCE: 4.7KM/2.9 MILES » **TOTAL ASCENT**: 661M/2,169FT » **START GR**: NN 234088 » **TIME**: ALLOW 4 HOURS
SATNAV: G83 7AS » **MAP**: OS EXPLORER OL39, LOCH LOMOND NORTH, 1:25,000 » **REFRESHMENTS**: OPTIONS IN ARROCHAR OR INVERARAY » **NAVIGATION**: GOOD PATH MOST OF THE WAY. STEEP SERIOUS TERRAIN. USE ALTERNATIVE DESCENT IN POOR VISIBILITY.

Directions – Beinn an Lochain

S→ From the lay-by, cross the crash barrier and **go down to the stream**. This can usually be crossed easily. When in spate it is better to cross a few metres to our left (south). This crossing spot uses a small grassy island. **Cross the stream**: jump on to the island and then jump across the narrowest section. Once across, head up and **right** on very boggy ground on a faint path. This is a great place for spotted orchids. Go past a prominent free-standing boulder, up and **right** in a deeply eroded path, steeply to the ridge.

2 **Once on the ridge** the path is clear and much less boggy! Cross numerous slabs and small rocky steps climbing steeply towards a short wall. Cross slabs, **left to right**, up this wall, until we are faced with a short **vertical section**. Holds are best on the right at a short corner. Another **short scramble** leads to a level section below a steep section with big crags running across the ridge. The path passes the top of a steep gully on our left, then goes **right** and up around steep boulders. The path becomes narrow and cuts across the steep grassy rake above the cliffs, now out of sight down to our right. Stay on the path and watch your footwork; slips here have ended in disaster. At the end of this traverse is a steep corner with easy scrambling above a very steep gully sweeping downwards and right. Another place for great care. **At no point in this entire section is it safe to deviate from the path**. Above this traverse, the path heads up and **left**. Take a moment to look back along the traverse path and make a mental note of the exit from the short scramble. If this point is not obvious in descent, in cloud or fog, it is safer to go back over the summit and descend the southern flanks of the hill rather than explore in the hope of finding the path.

3 Climb up and **left on the edge** above the upper band of steep crags then **turn right** and cross a level section. We can now see the final section of ridge. To the right is a big corrie, steep crags and a curiously balanced boulder, the Old Man's Face? This, last, section is narrow and hugs the right (northern) edge of the ridge with dizzying drops into the corrie below. The angle suddenly eases, and the summit appears! There is a small cairn where we can stop and admire the view. Ben Lomond in the south-east is just visible through Tarbet Glen. Moving clockwise, we can see The Brack with shy Ben Donich to its north-west. Further round are the hills above Loch Goil and Beinn Bheula. To the west, on a clear day we can see the Paps of Jura and, further north, Ben More on Mull. In the north-west we can make out the white buildings of Inveraray far below. Continuing north, we have Ben Cruachan, and then

11 Beinn An Lochain

Directions – Beinn an Lochain continued ...

our close neighbour Binnein an Fhìdhleir, just across Glen Kinglas. Then it is Beinn Ime, Beinn Luibhean and The Cobbler before arriving back to gaze down over Loch Restil to Rest and be Thankful.

4 **In good visibility, retrace your steps down the ridge**, taking great care to identify the start of the traverse path above the crags.

> **OR** **In poor visibility** it is safer to head **south** from the summit on a good path across a small subsidiary summit. Here the path passes small lochans and **descends the broad ridge**. Just beyond a broad lower top (834m; NN 217074) the now faint path swings to the **right** around some crags before turning back **left** and disappearing (NN 216072). The descent now follows steep, pathless terrain heading **east** towards the car park at Rest and be Thankful. Take care on this rough, ankle-testing, ground and head for the **left-hand (northern) side of the forest** below. The northern edge of the forest can be followed all the way down to the B828. **Turn left** to reach the A83. **Turn left** and walk back on the Loch Restil side of the A83 to the start point (it is a busy road; walk on the other side of the crash barrier to protect yourself from the traffic).

Notes: This walk is best as an out-and-back by the ridge route. Accidents have happened when people having missed the traverse above the crags, tried to descend steep grass and ultimately slipped over a crag. So, if in doubt, go down via the optional route to the south.

RAINBOW OVER LOCH RESTIL

LOOKING OVER THE SLOY DAM

12 Glen Loin & the Sloy Dam   21.9km/13.6 miles

An extended circuit of Glen Loin, Coiregrogain and the Sloy Dam, including lunch by the side of a Highland icon.

Arrochar » Glen Loin » Coiregrogain » Sloy Dam » Glen Loin » Arrochar

Start

Succoth car park, north of Arrochar (parking charge). GR: NN 295049. (Additional parking available at Loch Long car park (parking charge), 250m to the east on the A83. GR: NN 298049.)

The Walk

This is the longest walk in our little book of adventures. It is a different type of outing – we don't climb to a summit – but it does have a real high point. We start below tall conifers, so dense that light barely reaches the forest floor. Trees don't naturally grow so close to each other, but this forest is not natural, it is an industrialised tree factory. Water, another very abundant commodity, is also industrialised in these mountains. It is collected, trapped and then set free in order to extract the energy within.

Argyll has water in bucket loads. It falls from the sky, sometimes without pause, and cascades in great waterfalls down the steep hillsides. It washes away main roads and forms great puddles – our mighty freshwater lochs. It would be a shame to waste it. So, just after World War II, when the nation was on its knees, hydro power was seen as the fuel for the economic recovery of a broken nation and for the occasional kettle or two. Up high in the mountains above Loch Lomond there was a small wild loch, the loch of the MacFarlane battle cry … Loch Sloy. Over not much more than four years, and at the cost of 21 workers' lives, Loch Sloy was drilled, diverted and dammed. The output from the mighty dam channelled into four huge pipes running down the side of Ben Vorlich. All of this to wring out the energy contained in rain.

This long walk uses lots of energy, we need enough to propel us in a big circuit with an extension up to the great dam of Sloy. We will be amazed at what was built, so high in the mountains. Once across the dam we can sit and recharge our batteries with lunch high above our starting point … energising us for the return to sea level in Arrochar.

GLEN LOIN & THE SLOY DAM

DISTANCE: 21.9KM/13.6 MILES » **TOTAL ASCENT**: 717M/2,352FT » **START GR**: NN 295049 » **TIME**: ALLOW 6-8 HOURS
SATNAV: G83 7AP » **MAP**: OS EXPLORER OL39, LOCH LOMOND NORTH, 1:25,000 » **REFRESHMENTS**: ARROCHAR CHIPPY, BEN ARTHURS BOTHY OR THE VILLAGE INN, ARROCHAR » **NAVIGATION**: EASY FOREST ROADS AND TRAILS.

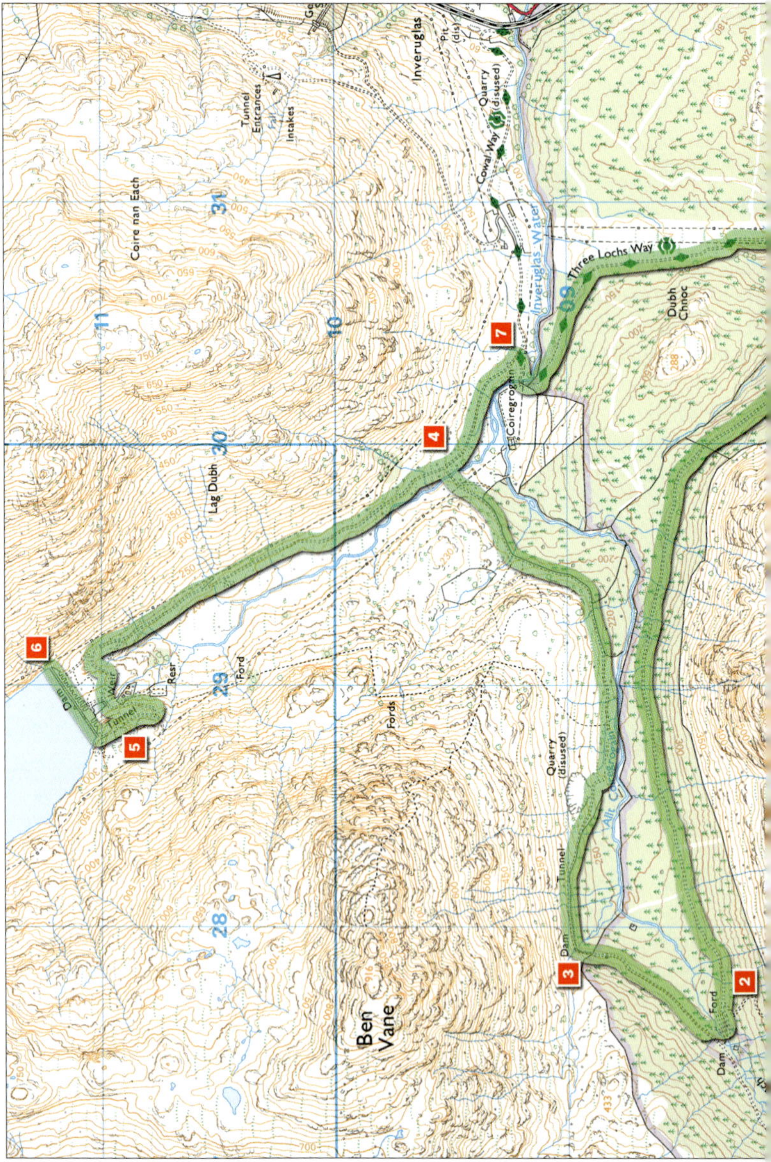

Inveruglas
Tunnel Entrances
Intakes
Coire nan Each
Cowal Way
Quarry (disused)
Inveruglas Water
Three Lochs Way
Dubh Chnoc
Coiregrogain
Lag Dubh
Resr
Ford
Fords
Tunnel
Dam
Quarry (disused)
Ben Vane
1
2
3
4
5
6
7

12 Glen Loin & the Sloy Dam

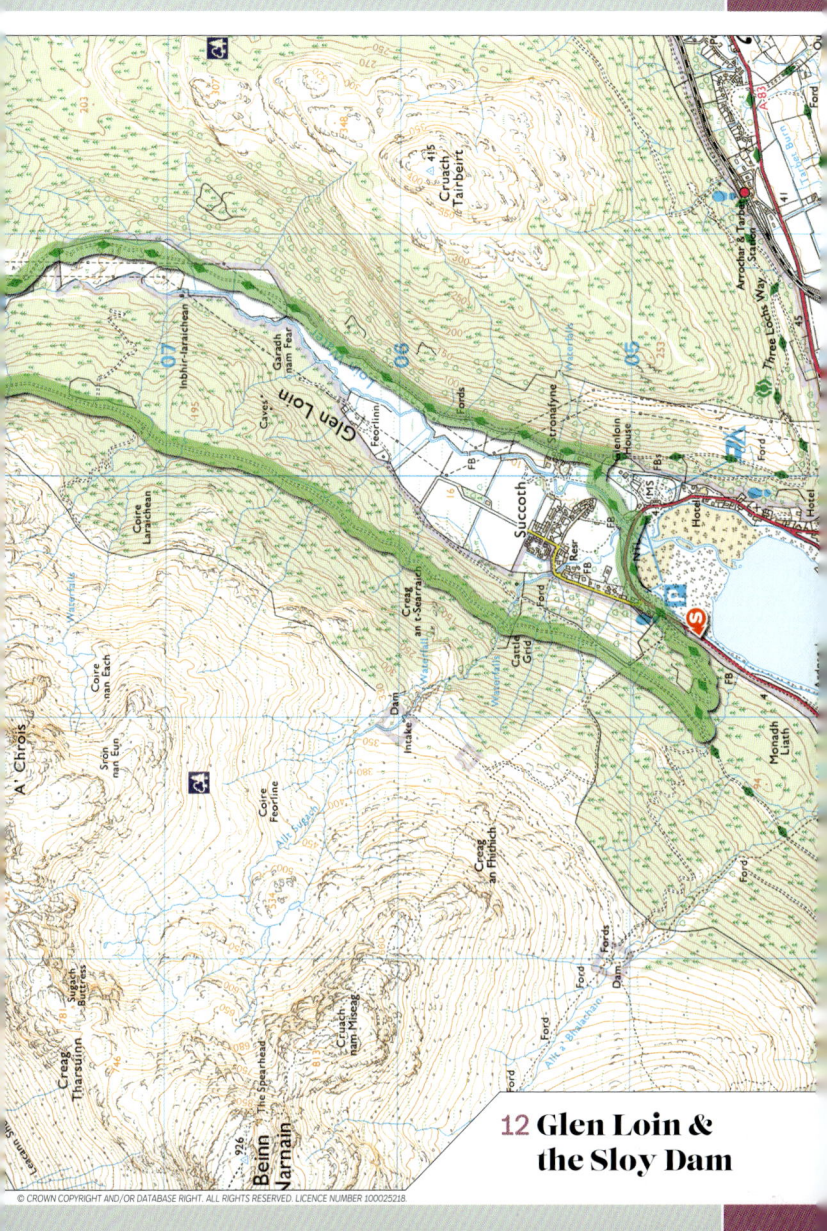

12 GLEN LOIN & THE SLOY DAM - **ARROCHAR ALPS**

Directions – Glen Loin & the Sloy Dam

S The path starts opposite Succoth car park. **Follow the zigzags** through the forest to a bench beside a forestry road. **Turn right**, heading north-east on the wide track. After about 600m, **fork left** at a signpost. Continue through the trees with occasional views to Ben Lomond to our south-east and to Ben Vorlich in the north. After 3km the track bends to the **left** (west) and heads into the Glen of Coiregrogain. Ahead we can see the eastern face of Beinn Ime.

2 A long straight section leads to a small dam, part of the Sloy collection system. Just before this small dam the path splits and we go **right** down the slope to the almost dry riverbed of the Allt Coiregrogain. Cross the ford and climb up through the trees to a junction with another wide track. **Turn right** (heading north-east), pass a derelict building on our left and soon arrive at a gate and stile.

3 **Cross the stile**; we can see a scenic waterfall ahead on our left. The waterfall has been harvested by a somewhat less scenic concrete dam, again part of the Sloy network. Views to the east are good here and we can look back south to the rugged slopes of A'Chrois, visible now that we have left the forest. Descend steeply on loose gravel and pass a disused quarry on the left. In the quarry is a large steel box, perhaps once used as a safe for the dynamite! The route continues down and around the south-east ridge of Ben Vane. Go **straight ahead** and cross a concrete bridge at a T-junction with the hydro road from Inveruglas. **Turn left** and head for our target – the Sloy Dam.

4 The road climbs steadily towards the dam with splendid views to Ben Vane on our left and to Ben Vorlich on our right. The road comes close to the right-hand end of the dam before swinging **left** and descending under the great buttresses of the dam wall. **Cross a small bridge** from where we can see the big valve at the bottom of the dam. Let's hope Robin the dam engineer doesn't open it until we are out of the firing line! The road climbs steeply in a series of hairpins to a tunnel through a cliff at the left-hand edge of the dam. Before the tunnel a flat grassy area is a magnificent viewpoint. We can see the dam walls jammed hard up against Ben Vane and Ben Vorlich – a real watertight finish.

5 **Go through the tunnel** and emerge to our first views of Loch Sloy. **Cross the dam**, looking left to the loch and right to the sloping buttresses – great fun. The loch surface is maintained at 859 feet (262 metres) above sea level. At the far end of the dam on Ben Vorlich a trig point sits on top of a small crag. Climb up to this for lunch with views of the loch, mountains and of course the mighty dam itself. Although not a summit, this trig point is a great place to take in the views. To the south we can see the shapely A'Chrois. Moving clockwise, we see the rugged flanks of Ben Vane then our eyes are drawn along Loch Sloy, its north-west extremity framed between Beinn Dubh to the left and Ben Vorlich to the right. Further around we look up Ben Vorlich on which we are perched. Next look east along the glen across Loch Lomond towards Loch Arklet above Inversnaid. Almost all the way around now and before we return to A'Chrois we see the squat rounded hill of Cruach Tairbeirt sitting above our descent path.

6 Either descend directly from the trig point towards the road below the dam using a steep stoney path or, if we haven't had enough of the dam and the tunnel, go back across and retrace our steps. Once on the hydro road, continue **straight ahead** at the T-junction at the low bridge that we passed earlier. Head toward Inveruglas for about 500m until a signposted path junction.

7 **Turn right**, heading towards Arrochar. **Cross a bridge** then **go left through a gate** and follow the narrow path once more into a tall forest. The path here is rough and narrow with lots of bracken in the summer. Eventually we arrive at a great viewpoint right beside a pylon! The path descends steeply to the **left** before reaching the floor of Glen Loin. **Cross a small bridge** and then **go through a gate** (with a *Cowal Way* waymarker); follow the path through mixed woodland. At a path junction (where the left-hand fork goes to the train station), **fork right**, heading steeply downwards, pass a house and then head straight across a field on a broad track to the road out of Glen Loin. **Turn left** (with the river on your right) to reach the main road in Arrochar and **turn right** to return to the car park … phew! By now we have walked over 20km and will need refreshment; having seen enough water for one day perhaps we can find something stronger?

Notes: This route could be shortened by omitting the visit to the dam, but what would be the point in that? Or, it could be done in the opposite direction, but the views in Glen Loin are superior in descent. If you don't fancy such a big walk, then the dam can be visited by a much shorter out-and-back walk from Inveruglas.

ON THE NORTH-EAST RIDGE OF BEN DONICH

13 Ben Donich

6.6km/4.1 miles

A short, varied outing with views worthy of a clear day!

B828 parking area » Forestry road » Coire Culach » Ben Donich » Coire Culach » Forestry road » B828 parking area

Start
Parking area on the southern side of the B828, south of Rest and be Thankful. GR: NN 228070.

The Walk

Ben Donich is a curious hill. Prominent from nowhere really; I cannot ever remember standing on another summit and saying 'oh look there's Ben Donich'. I first climbed it almost 40 years ago in torrential rain and cloud. As a result of that miserable ascent, it took me 36 years to return! When I did go back it was a revelation. On a nice day this hill is an ideal short outing, offering mixed terrain, easy scrambling and views which are second to none.

Ben Donich is Gaelic for 'evil mountain' and I used to wonder why it had such a negative name. On a recent winter ascent, I found out! The path winds up the northern ridge and it snakes around some deep slots and holes. These fissures are right beside the path and careful inspection shows that some are deep enough to swallow you whole! So, one winter day, after heavy snowfall I found myself, solo, breaking trail through knee-deep powder in billowing cloud and mist. I was enjoying the fact that no one had been up since the snowfall, when I realised that I was close to these big holes. I became very aware that I was in the Scottish equivalent of a heavily crevassed glacier and that one wrong step could break a leg or, worse, send me to the bowels of the Earth, never to return. I began to feel very scared. Sensing 'evil' all around I turned and headed back in my footprints, defeated by little Ben Donich.

Take my advice: choose a clear, dry day and stick to the path. Be prepared for a little bit of easy scrambling near the top and bring a nice lunch for the summit views down the Argyll sea lochs. All very pleasant and benign, just don't fall down an evil slot ...

BEN DONICH

DISTANCE: 6.6KM/4.1 MILES » **TOTAL ASCENT**: 576M/1,890FT » **START GR**: NN 228070 » **TIME**: ALLOW 4 HOURS
SATNAV: G83 7AS » **MAP**: OS EXPLORER OL39, LOCH LOMOND NORTH, 1:25,000 » **REFRESHMENTS**: OPTIONS IN ARROCHAR OR INVERARAY » **NAVIGATION**: GOOD PATH MOST OF THE WAY. SOME EASY SCRAMBLING.

Directions – Ben Donich

S From the parking area walk along the forestry track to reach a signpost on the left. **Turn left**, following the sign for *Ben Donich*. Climb **south** through a wooded area to join the northern ridge of Ben Donich. Go through a gate and follow the path round to the **right** across a boggy area then up and **left on to the ridge**.

2 **Continue along the ridge**. The path crosses some smooth slabs of schist as it heads up the ridge; note the slots and evil holes either side of the route! The ridge steepens up ahead. To our right are splendid views of the chaotic boulderfields of the northern corrie. The path goes steeply up and **left** before swinging back **right** around more deep holes.

3 We arrive at the top of a small crag. Looking down, we can see the path crossing boulders and crags in a heavily 'crevassed' zone 15m below. The path seems to just stop at the top of this downclimb. This is the route; alternatives either side are potentially dangerous. **Climb down carefully on the polished schist**. At the foot of the scramble, **follow the path over boulders** and step across some very big holes. The next section **crosses a steep wall**, going right to left on a narrow path, then things level off as we approach the summit.

4 Ben Donich's trig point has recently had a lick of paint! Let's admire the views. To the north we can see Beinn an Lochain. Moving clockwise, we see Beinn Luibhean and Beinn Ime then, further round, the southern peak of The Cobbler. To the east, we see Ben Lomond, The Brack and Cnoc Coinnich. Continuing round, our eyes are drawn downwards along the fjords of Argyll. Far below, Loch Goil runs south to join forces with Loch Long before spilling into the Firth of Clyde. On a clear day, Arran and Ailsa Craig are easily spotted, and on a very clear day you might even see the coast of Northern Ireland. As we return to our starting position, the Cruachan Range is visible in the distance. Those are the highlights but there are other hills to name in between. **Retrace your steps** to return to the start. The short scramble feels much easier this time and we are soon enjoying the splendid open views. The finest view is of Beinn an Lochain and the lovely little Loch Restil at its foot. Wind carefully through the evil crevassed zone and then along the track to the car park.

Notes: This out-and-back walk could easily be linked up with The Brack (walk 14) to form a fine traverse. This link-up requires a long walk up the forest track in Glen Croe to get back to the start point.

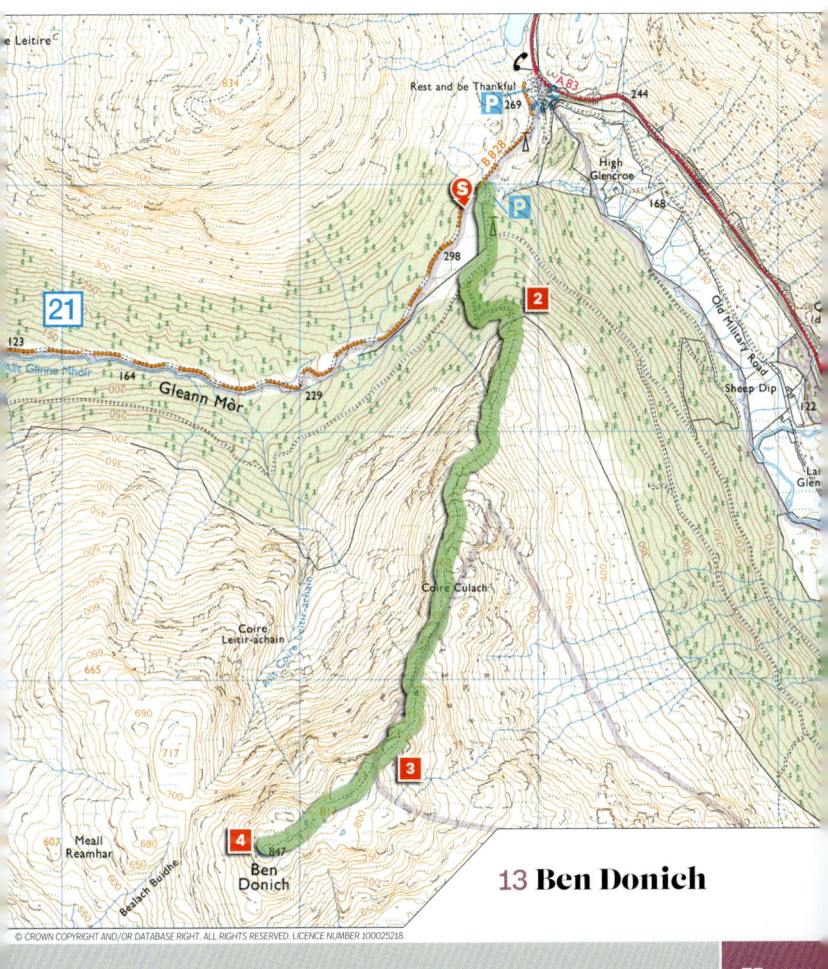

13 Ben Donich

LOOKING TOWARDS GLEN CROE FROM THE BRACK

14 The Brack

6.9km/4.3 miles

Enjoy steep and rough trails on this seldom-frequented Corbett.

Ardgartan » Forestry road » Bealach » The Brack » Bealach » Forestry road » Ardgartan

Start
Ardgartan car park. GR: NN 269037.

The Walk
Most of the routes in this book are on excellent, wide and, in some cases, restored paths. The Brack is an exception. This walk uses a deeply-eroded, muddy and discontinuous trench. In all but the most sustained drought the levels of mud and general slipperiness encountered here are second to none. So why bother? The Brack is one of the quietest Corbetts in the region and you have a greater chance of solitude here than on almost any other route in this guidebook. It is a complex mountain with towering crags forming its east and south-east ramparts and a steep, grassy, boulder-filled corrie, which we will use for our ascent.

The cliffs, best viewed from the car park at Rest and be Thankful, are home to numerous climbs. Popular with Victorian mountaineers, dressed in tweeds and carrying hemp ropes, these climbs were neglected until they were recently rediscovered as hard winter test pieces. We will settle for a look at them as we plug up the rough, wild corrie. We might even be lucky enough to see the eagle who sometimes soars above the crags.

The Brack's strange name is probably an Anglicisation of the Gaelic *breac*, meaning 'dappled' or 'speckled', due to the mountain's mixture of heather, rock, boulders and well, let's face it, mud! Once we reach the upper ridge of the mountain the walking is splendid, with lochans, crags and views all around. Pick a dry day, expect to work hard for this summit and wear your gaiters.

THE BRACK

DISTANCE: 6.9KM/4.3 MILES » **TOTAL ASCENT**: 753M/2,470FT » **START GR**: NN 269037 » **TIME**: ALLOW 5 HOURS
SATNAV: G83 7AS » **MAP**: OS EXPLORER OL39, LOCH LOMOND NORTH, 1:25,000 » **REFRESHMENTS**: OPTIONS IN ARROCHAR OR INVERARAY » **NAVIGATION**: FAIRLY EASY, BUT PATH DISCONTINUOUS IN PLACES.

Directions – The Brack

S From the car park, go **north-west** along the forestry road. After about 700m pass a small cottage on the right then continue for 1km. Soon we see our objective towering above the trees. The forestry road curves sharply to the **left** to reach a T-junction with signs for mountain bike trails.

2 **Turn right** and after 100m **turn left**, following a signpost for *The Brack*. Surely some mistake! At the start of the path, we are confronted with **steep, tricky scrambling** over near-vertical boulders. The boulders are smooth and slippery and the path is undercut, creating two challenging obstacles. Forget rock climbing ethics and just thrutch up these steep sections, grabbing the thick, convenient and well-used tree roots as they appear at eye level. Above this, the **path continues steeply through dense forest** and we gain height quickly. Near the top of the forest section there is an area of exceptionally high-quality mud just before a dilapidated fence and a white post. **Cross the fence** and follow the path up a spur with excellent views of the cliffs above and to the right.

3 The steep and narrow path is easily followed until it **swings to the right** (west) and **descends to a pool** above a small waterfall. **Cross to the western side of the burn** and go steeply up the ridge towards the corrie above. At this point take a breather and enjoy the views up Glen Croe. We get closer and closer to the burn and at one point the path is steep and loose. A slip here would likely end up in the burn so be careful. The path heads away from the burn before **curving left** and becoming less distinct. The gradient here is easier and the path becomes broken. Take the line of least bogginess heading **south towards the bealach**.

4 On the bealach the views really open up. **Head west around a lovely lochan** nestled beneath some big boulders. The path **winds right**, heading steeply across the hillside before heading into a narrow corrie. At the top of this small corrie cross a ridge and **turn right** (north) into a near identical narrow corrie. The steep path leads directly to the summit with its trig pillar. The views are spectacular: facing east we can see our faithful beacon, Ben Lomond. Moving clockwise we can see the hills to the east of Loch Long, leading to the Firth of Clyde. To the south-west are the mountains of Arran and Ailsa Craig; Cnoc Coinnich is very close by. To the north-west, Ben Donich is its usual shy self and, continuing clockwise, we see Beinn an Lochain, Binnein an Fhìdhleir and then Beinn Luibhean, Beinn Ime and The Cobbler form an arc above

Glen Croe. Finally, we have Beinn Narnain, with its strikingly flat summit. Splendid stuff!

5 We **re-trace our steps** to descend. Pass the lochan then **turn left at the bealach**. It is worth pausing to look up to the cliffs and steep gullies to our left. Is that a raven, or a buzzard ... or even an eagle? Walk down through the forest to reach the forestry road; **turn right** then **turn left** at the T-junction to return to the car park.

Notes: This route could easily be linked with Cnoc Coinnich & The Steeple (walk 16) to form a traverse. This traverse requires two cars or a pick-up and drop-off, in Coilessan Glen or Lochgoilhead. Or we could link with Ben Donich (walk 13), giving a longer day with a lengthy walk back down the forestry roads to our start point. Or of course do all three!

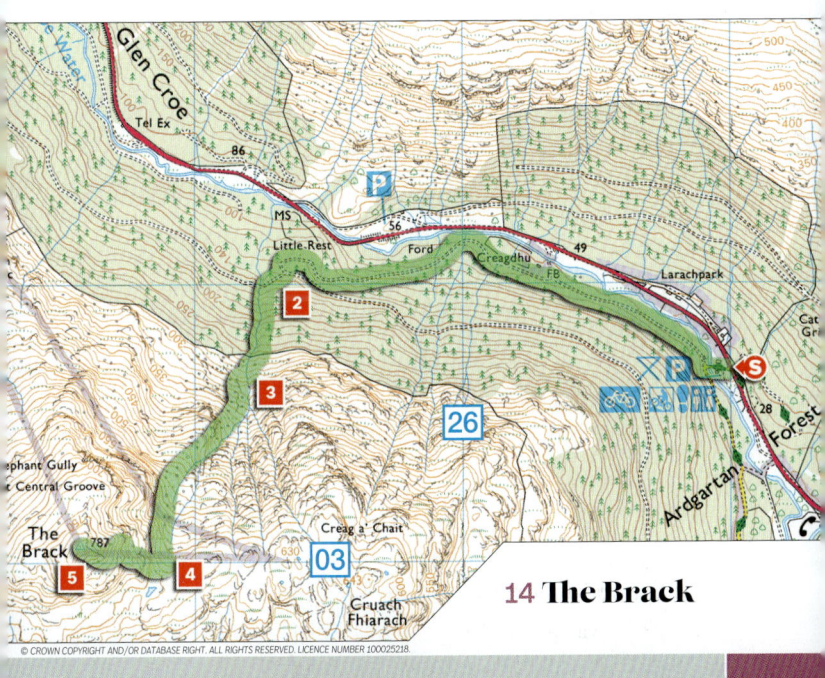

14 The Brack

A'CHROIS FROM THE BEN VANE PATH

15 Ben Vane

11.2km/7 miles

A steep climb at the centre of the Arrochar Alps.

Inveruglas » Hydro road » Bridge » Ben Vane » Bridge » Hydro road » Inveruglas

Start
Inveruglas car park (parking charge).
GR: NN 323099.

The Walk
Often you have to use your imagination to see how a hill earned its Gaelic name, but not on this occasion. Ben Vane is the Anglicisation of *Ben Mheadhoin* ('Mh' is pronounced 'V'), meaning 'middle hill'. Approaching today's target, it is obvious that this little boulder of a Munro is slap-bang in the middle – in the heart of the Arrochar Alps.

Today's walk is an 'out-and-back'; the alternatives being long and arduous link-ups. Ben Vane is strenuous enough for a short summer outing. The hill is unusually, and consistently, steep. After a walk up a tarmac road blighted by ugly pylons, we launch up a steep, scrambly ascent of the eastern ridge then enjoy an undulating (are we there yet?) rocky summit ridge. Once we get high enough above the wee, steep corrie, we can look down on the great dam on Loch Sloy.

On the way back we get to do it all again, this time enjoying the brilliant views that were behind us on the way up. As the ground steepens and as the sweat beads on our foreheads, we can motivate ourselves with the battle-cry of the local Clan MacFarlane ... 'Loch Sloy'!

BEN VANE

DISTANCE: 11.2KM/7 MILES » **TOTAL ASCENT**: 871M/2,858FT » **START GR**: NN 323099 » **TIME**: ALLOW 5-6 HOURS
SATNAV: G83 7DP » **MAP**: OS EXPLORER OL39, LOCH LOMOND NORTH, 1:25,000 » **REFRESHMENTS**: SEASONAL CAFE IN INVERUGLAS CAR PARK » **NAVIGATION**: GOOD PATHS; SOME VERY EASY SCRAMBLING.

Directions – Ben Vane

S From the car park, **turn left** on to the A82. **Cross the road** by the power station, walking south on the western side of the carriageway on a good path, signposted for the *Cowal Way* and the *Three Lochs Way*. Notice the pipes from the power station running down Ben Vorlich – they are a local icon. Tour guides tell the more gullible tourists that Sloy and its pipes are part of the Loch Lomond Haggis Factory! After about 700m we reach an **access road on the right** with a gate festooned with *no parking* signs.

2 **Go through the gate** and walk along the road. **Pass under the green viaduct** for the West Highland Line. Where the railings on the left stop, there is a shortcut through the woods; ignore this, it doesn't help. Just carry on along the tarmac road as it **curves to the right** and climbs steadily.

3 After a stiff pull up the road arrive at an industrial scene with pylons and a futuristic substation building on the left. **Ignore** a road going off to the right. Carry on **straight ahead** towards the foreshortened eastern ridge of Ben Vane.

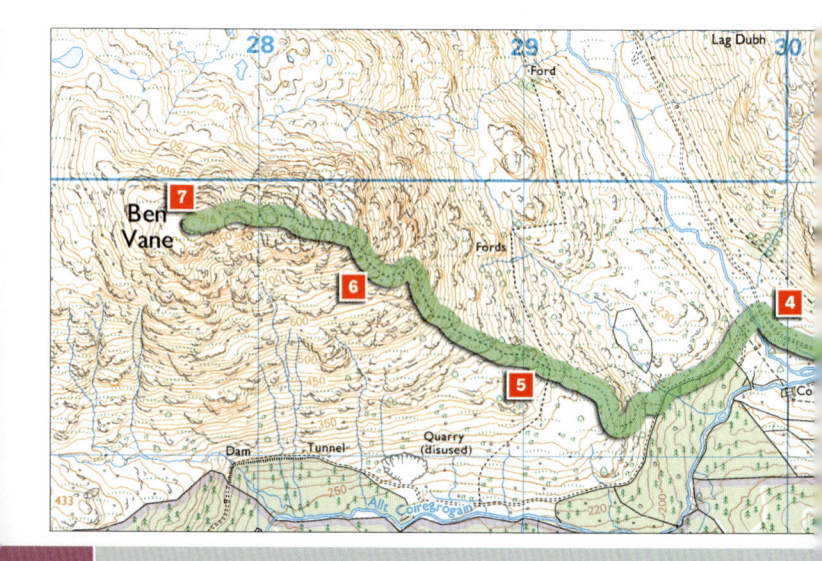

DAY WALKS IN LOCH LOMOND & THE TROSSACHS

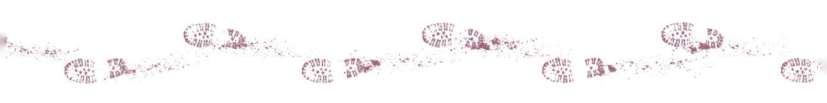

4 The road splits at a low concrete bridge (NN 299095). **Go left across the bridge**. Soon we cross another small, older, bridge where a stream passes under the road. A path starts on the right (north side) of this burn near some rowan trees; **ignore** this path (it is the old path leading across some boggy ground). 50 metres further on (NN 295092), **turn right** on to the new path heading towards the ridge. Go up the steep lower ridge with splendid views of A'Chrois to the south. The path crosses a flat bog and heads towards the main part of the ridge.

5 **Continue up the ridge**. From now on the steepness is unrelenting and the views ahead are limited to the ridge itself. Above and to the left on the ridge a prominent rocky overhang forms a shallow cave. This overhang is a good place to shelter on rainy days, perhaps for some food and to put on some layers before the upper mountain. Follow the path up and round to the **right** across steep rocky slopes. Hands are needed occasionally for balance, but it is all simple enough. On open slopes above head up and round to the **left**. The views down to Loch Sloy on the right are excellent. The ridge continues over numerous small rocky steps requiring simple scrambling; stick to the path and where there is more than one path it is generally easier on the right.

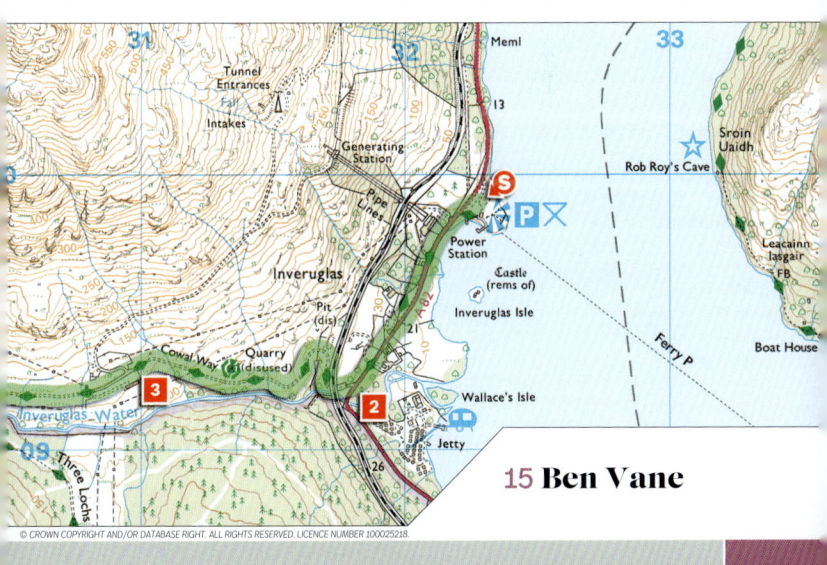

15 Ben Vane

Directions – Ben Vane continued ...

6 The summit seems elusive as we wind through numerous crags. Sometimes it feels that we are 'in' the ridge rather than on it! Near the top a band of steep slabs blocks our way. The path starts at the bottom right and **slopes up and left across these slabs**. The best route leaves this left-sloping path 6 metres after the start on an eroded track going up and **right** to the ridge. The summit plateau is gained with its big cairn at the western end and sometimes a small lochan forms in a hollow on top. Now at last we can appreciate the views. To the south-east we can see Ben Lomond; turning clockwise we have A'Chrois, then the strikingly flat summit of Beinn Narnain, The Cobbler's jagged central peak and then across the Bealach a'Mhaim, Beinn Ime and Beinn Chorranach. Continuing round, we can see Beinn an Lochain, and even the distant Paps of Jura are visible on a clear day. Further round we come to a distant view of Ben More on Mull, then Ben Vorlich fills the view above Loch Sloy. Turning back towards our starting position we look across Loch Lomond to Inversnaid. Loch Arklet was once part of an ancient river system, flowing west to east, which linked Loch Sloy with Loch Katrine. This ancient river was severed by the glaciers that dug out the Loch Lomond trench.

7 To descend, we **retrace our steps**. The character of the descent is entirely different. The views are expansive to the east, a nice contrast to the upward views which were mainly of hillside in front of our noses!

Notes: This hill is steep, rough and studded with crags and gullies, so stick to the path or things could get tricky. Linking Ben Vane with other mountains in the Arrochar Alps is a big day and, due to forestry, careful map work is required to avoid long detours.

THE ROAD TO BEN VANE

THE ALLT AIRIGH NA CREIGE

16 Cnoc Coinnich & The Steeple — 9.8km/6.1 miles

A rough, challenging circuit above Lochgoilhead.

Lochgoilhead » Glen Donich » Cnoc Coinnich » The Steeple » Lochgoilhead

Start
Car park in Lochgoilhead.
GR: NN 200013.

The Walk

For a long time Cnoc Coinnich was a neglected mountain. Then in 2016 a geographical survey discovered that the summit was a metre higher than previously measured. It might not seem much, but those extra 100 centimetres were enough to catapult this lowly hill into the big league – overnight Cnoc Coinnich became a Corbett! With the newfound status came walkers keen to bag the top, and on the hillside this traffic has started to create a faint trail.

The hill sits south of The Brack, above a bealach which marks the high point of a crossing from Loch Long in the east to Lochgoilhead in the west. This hill pass is now part of the Cowal Way, a long-distance path that allows the Cnoc to be accessed from either lochside. The Coilessan route (from Loch Long) has recently suffered from industrial forestry and is much less scenic as a result. We will use the Lochgoilhead approach which allows a circuit taking in the striking little summit of The Steeple.

This route has a bit of everything. We start off on forest tracks, pass waterfalls and then follow muddy, faint trails on open hillside before traversing a rough, pathless high moor. The Steeple is a cracking viewpoint and once it is gained a path reappears for the descent. The walking is hard, but the views are excellent and the reward of two rocky summits makes it all worthwhile. The descent from Cnoc Coinnich towards The Steeple involves very steep ground with crags and potentially hazardous terrain, so care is needed.

What can we say about Cnoc Coinnich, our celebrity Corbett? Well this hill is one of surprises; it starts off, as its name suggests, a mossy lump, but as we gain height it reveals dramatic cliffs and a rocky summit. The top is a flat slab and when I was last there, I measured the height of the cairn at, roughly, one metre. I wonder …

CNOC COINNICH & THE STEEPLE

DISTANCE: 9.8KM/6.1 MILES » **TOTAL ASCENT**: 790M/2,592FT » **START GR**: NN 200013 » **TIME**: ALLOW 5-7 HOURS
SATNAV: PA24 8AQ » **MAP**: OS EXPLORER OL37, COWAL EAST, 1:25,000 » **REFRESHMENTS**: THE BOAT SHED CAFE, LOCHGOILHEAD » **NAVIGATION**: FOREST PATHS AND OPEN HILLSIDE; TRICKY NAVIGATION FROM CNOC COINNICH TO THE STEEPLE.

POSTS SHOW THE WAY UP TO CNOC COINNICH

16 Cnoc Coinnich & The Steeple

89

Directions – Cnoc Coinnich & The Steeple

S **Cross the road** towards the little white Post Office and walk a few metres to the **north** (left). A road heads east between houses and is signposted *Loch Lomond and Cowal Way*. **Turn right** along this narrow street with views of The Steeple up on our right. The road narrows and **swings left to a gate** with warnings that we are about to cross a field which is home to Highland cattle – dog walkers take note. Continue to another gate and a signpost; **turn left**, following the signpost for *Glen Donich*, up the broad forest track. In just over 1km **ignore** a path heading south-east off to the right. Follow marker posts and go through another gate into the forest. Behind us we can see Beinn Bheula across Loch Goil.

2 Arrive at a series of waterfalls and wooden footbridges across Donich Water and Allt Airigh na Creige; this is a lovely spot to pause for a while. **Cross the bridge** over the Allt Airigh na Creige; **ignore** a path going off to the left, instead take the **right fork** and climb very steeply uphill, this will have you puffing! In 700m we come to a broad clearing in the forest with a signpost. Take the wide firebreak heading up and **right** (east). The route is marked with tall white wooden posts. Follow the path uphill, alongside a burn. There are wooden benches if a rest is needed. The path leads to open hillside. The path here is boggy and indistinct, but the white posts continue. After another bench, go through a gate and follow the posts across the hillside.

3 Just before the bealach a faint path breaks off to the **right**, over boggy ground towards the north-west ridge of Cnoc Coinnich. There are splendid views towards The Brack and through Coilessan Glen to the hills above Loch Long. **Head up the ridge** on the discontinuous path on easy mossy slopes. An impressive crag is avoided by slopes on its **right** (west). Another steep rise leads to the flat summit platform with steep crags on the left (east). The summit is marked with a low cairn – a good place to take in the views. To the north is the bulk of Ben Donich, its usual unimpressive self. Moving clockwise, we can see the southern peak of The Cobbler and closer to us is The Brack. Continuing on, the unmistakeable Ben Lomond lies beyond Tarbet Glen. The hills to the east of Loch Long, in particular Tullich Hill and Doune Hill, look shapely. Look on down the Clyde Sea Lochs, past the submarine base and out into the Clyde Estuary. To the south, Beinn Reithe (one for another day) looks very close, then the Cowal Hills fill the foreground. Next, we can see Beinn Bheula, just across Loch Goil. Look carefully for the summit rocks of our next objective, The Steeple, to the west. Back towards our starting point the view below is dominated by the massive holiday park at Lochgoilhead.

The hills to the west of Rest and be Thankful lead us back to the start. Quite a few there for future outings in Argyll!

4 In poor weather or if you have had enough, simply retrace the ascent route. To visit The Steeple, we now have some rough walking. In good visibility **head down the south-west ridge** of Cnoc Coinnich, taking great care to wind between the steep cliffs on broad grassy slopes to reach the **bealach** between Cnoc Coinnich and Beinn Reithe.

> **OR** **If visibility is poor**, we can reach this point by first going back down our **ascent route**. Once below and north-west of the summit rocks of Cnoc Coinnich, **turn left** and head south to contour below the summit buttresses.

5 From the broad bealach, head **north-west** on pathless, heathery terrain. Cross a small hump (387m), go across another bump (Tom nan Gamhna) and then descend steep, heathery slopes to a fence running across the hillside. Cross the fence at a **gate**, go up and then down another hillock then descend steeply into the gap east of the The Steeple. Once in this gap **turn right** (north) and pick up a faint path leading up and **left** to the summit. What a great viewpoint this is. At the south-west end of the summit is a big rocky platform with views down the length of Loch Goil. We can see straight down to the village and the car park below.

6 Head **north** from the summit on a path which eventually swings **left** (north-west) across the moor towards a lower rocky platform with great views down to the loch. The path is now well defined as it turns **left** and descends to a small buttress. This crag is equipped with anchor bolts for the local outdoor centre to teach climbing and abseiling. The path goes steeply down and **left**, beside a burn, passes under the crag then heads round to the **right**. Soon we reach a junction with the main track above the field where the cattle live. **Turn left** and go back to our starting point.

Notes: This is a strenuous walk that needs good visibility and some map reading to find the best route. The maps do not show the steep serious nature of the area south of the summit of Cnoc Coinnich. If in doubt, use the optional route described above. When forestry work has been completed the Coilessan approach from the east may once again be worth a visit.

THE SPEARHEAD BUTTRESS, BEINN NARNAIN

17 Beinn Narnain

11.8km/7.3 miles

A climb to the very tip of the spear of Beinn Narnain.

Arrochar » NN 281051 » South-east ridge » Cruach nam Miseag » Beinn Narnain » Bealach a' Mhaim » Narnain Boulders » NN 281051 » Arrochar

Start

Succoth car park, north of Arrochar (parking charge). GR: NN 295049. (Additional parking available at Loch Long car park (parking charge), 250m to the east on the A83. GR: NN 298049.)

The Walk

Beinn Narnain, one of the highest mountains in the Arrochar Alps, is massively upstaged by its smaller, show-off neighbour, The Cobbler. Both mountains are chips off the same block, but the massive bulk of Beinn Narnain more successfully resisted the forces of erosion and so its profile is less wild. Starting at sea level on the shores of Loch Long, it is a stiff climb to gain the 926-metre summit.

Beinn Narnain means 'notched or slotted mountain', perhaps due to the presence of deep rocky clefts on the south-east ridge, like those on Ben Donich (walk 13). These deep holes have caused serious accidents, but are easily avoided by sticking to the path. The summit lies just beyond the dramatic Spearhead buttress, a great prow of rock which is a splendid viewing platform on which to have lunch.

During the COVID-19 pandemic the hills were off-limits for three long months in the spring and summer of 2020. On the first day that restrictions were lifted I set off up Beinn Narnain. I had the mountain to myself until just below The Spearhead, where I met some angry residents. When no one had been able to visit the hills a 're-wilding' had occurred. A family of ptarmigan had taken up residence on the path at its narrowest point! Six fluffy chicks scuttled around my feet as mother and father ptarmigan hissed and flapped at me. Not wanting to step on a chick or beat off attacking parents, I showed them due respect and went around via steep ground to the east.

Choose a nice day. Save lunch for the top of The Spearhead and with luck you will have this route to yourself. If you see the ptarmigan family, send them my regards!

BEINN NARNAIN

DISTANCE: 11.8KM/7.3 MILES » **TOTAL ASCENT**: 975M/3,199FT » **START GR**: NN 295049 » **TIME**: ALLOW 6 HOURS
SATNAV: G83 7AP » **MAP**: OS EXPLORER OL39, LOCH LOMOND NORTH, 1:25,000 » **REFRESHMENTS**: ARROCHAR CHIPPY, BEN ARTHURS BOTHY OR THE VILLAGE INN, ARROCHAR » **NAVIGATION**: GOOD PATHS; SOME VERY EASY SCRAMBLING.

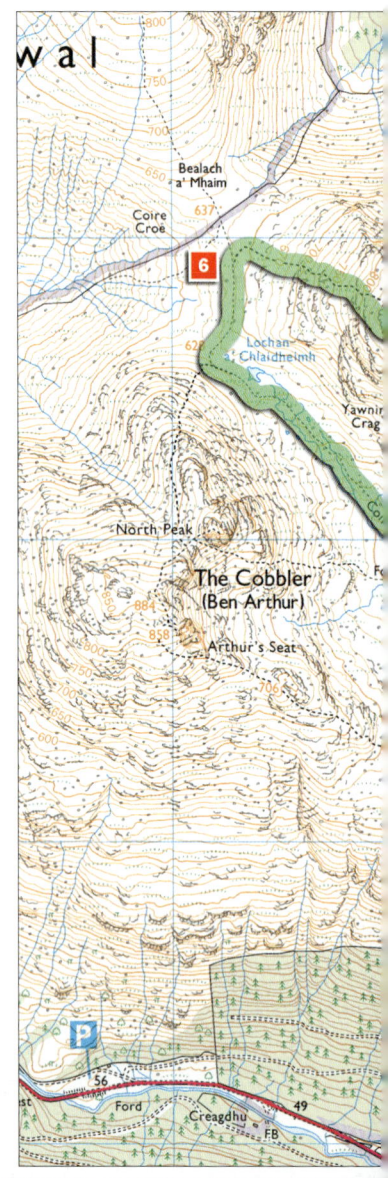

THE SPEARHEAD BUTTRESS

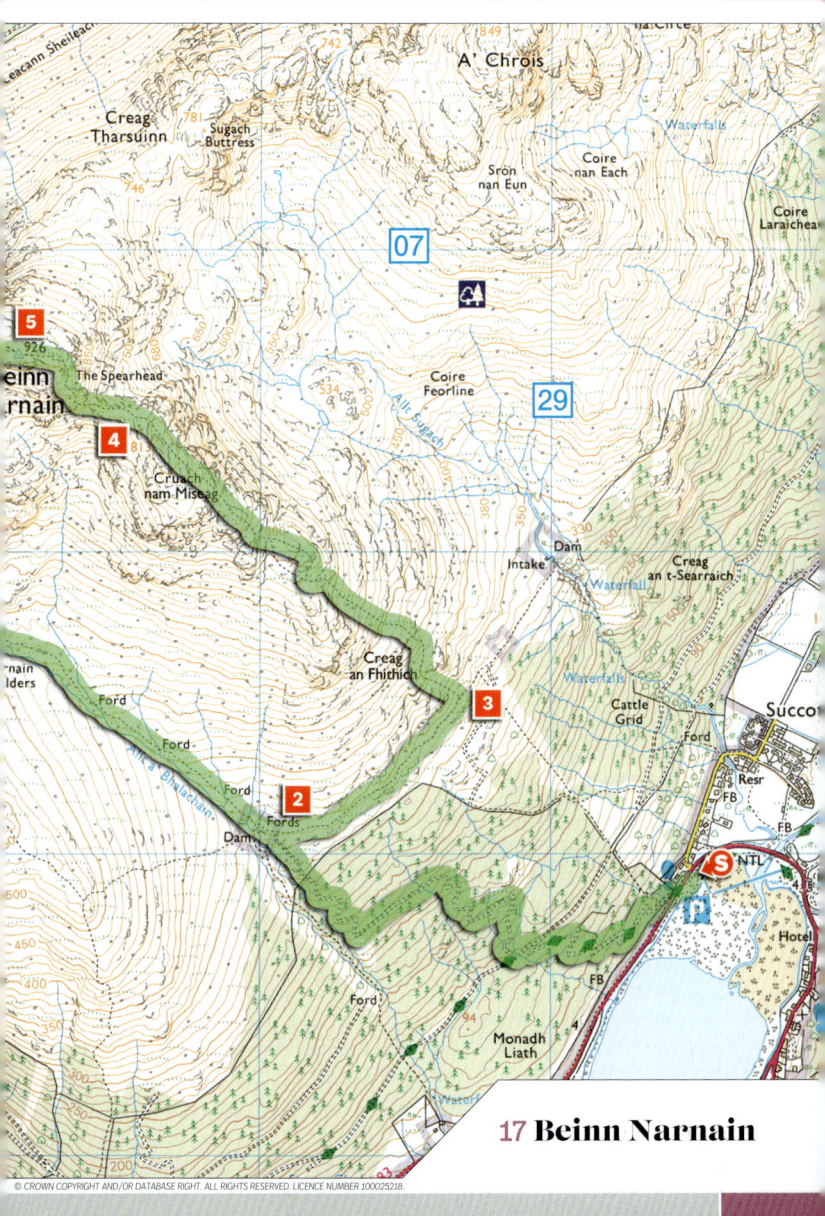

17 Beinn Narnain

Directions – Beinn Narnain

S▶ The path starts opposite Succoth car park. **Follow the zigzags** through the forest to a bench beside a forestry road. **Turn left** towards an antenna. Before the antenna **turn right** on to a signposted path, heading uphill. This path goes steeply through the forest then on to the open hillside.

2 At a level spot after we leave the forest (NN 281051; 340m) take the narrow path to the **right**, heading north-east. The path is nearly horizontal for most of the way to the start of the south-east ridge of Beinn Narnain.

3 After about 800m on this path **stone steps lead up and left** to the ridge. Head up towards Cruach nam Miseag. To our left are great views down Loch Long and to the right into Coire Feorline and to A'Chrois. Just above Cruach nam Miseag the path winds through crags before levelling off. As we crest the ridge, The Cobbler appears at eye level dead ahead. Continue **straight ahead** on the now rougher path, then **descend to the bealach**.

4 Immediately after the bealach the path narrows and steepens. Go **left** around some big crags. Hands are needed for short sections around some steep drops down to the left, so take care. Climb into a shallow corrie filled with a chaotic jumble of massive rocks beneath the towering Spearhead buttress. Follow a narrow trail up and very close to the right-hand flank of the buttress. The path goes into a gully with **steep scrambling** moves for a few metres. (The left-hand side of the gully is The Spearhead buttress.) The gully is steep, but it is short, and the holds are good. At the top a very short scramble leads on to the flat top of The Spearhead. Wet schist is very slippery, and the sides of the buttress are sheer – not a place for a slip or stumble! On a dry day it is a grandstand upon which to eat lunch while taking in the views. If the top of The Spearhead does not appeal or common sense prevails on a wet day, the summit lies just a few metres to the north-west. From the trig point, look south-east to Ben Lomond. Moving clockwise we have the eastern rampart of Loch Long, Ben Reoch, Tullich Hill and, further right, the Luss Hills. To the west we look down Loch Long to the sea, Arran and Ailsa Craig. Continuing round, we can see The Brack and The Cobbler. Then round to Beinn an Lochain, Beinn Luibhean, Beinn Ime and onwards to Ben Vane. Completing our circuit, we pass A'Chrois and then turn back past The Spearhead.

5 Take the path **west** from the trig point and go **slightly left** into a boulderfield. The path disappears in the jumble of rocks so just keep going down and **right**. (The path reappears at the far right side of the boulders.) Follow the path down the broad western ridge to the junction on Bealach a' Mhaim.

6 **Turn left** at the junction. After 300m **turn left** and head south-east back towards Arrochar. We pass the marker post for The Cobbler path and then the Narnain Boulders. Follow the main trail down through the forest to the car park.

Notes: The Bealach a' Mhaim is a major junction in the Arrochar Alps. It can be used to link Beinn Narnain with Beinn Ime and The Cobbler.

BEINN NARNAIN TRIG POINT AND BEN LOMOND

Section 4

The Northern Hills

Lying to the north and north-east of Loch Lomond & the Trossachs National Park is an extensive tract of rugged land packed tight with high peaks. In this area the hills are noticeably bigger, none more so than Ben More, the 'big hill'. Here our outings need to be planned carefully in anything but perfect weather. In this landscape there are fewer lochs to look down upon and, in general, there is a wilder, more committing feel to days spent among these peaks.

ON STOB BINNEIN (ROUTE 18)

GLEN DOCHART AND STRATH FILLAN FROM THE SLOPES OF BEN MORE (ROUTE 18)

LOCH LOMOND & THE TROSSACHS – SECTION 4

101

THE SLOPES OF BEN MORE

18 Ben More & Stob Binnein

9.6km/6 miles

Traverse these twin giants above Crianlarich.

Benmore Farm » Ben More » Bealach-eadar-dha Bheinn » Stob Binnein » Bealach-eadar-dha Bheinn » Benmore Glen » Benmore Farm

Start

A85, 50m east of Benmore Farm. GR: NN 414259. Roadside parking on the south side of the A85 (east of the farm) or in large lay-by 700m north-east on the north side of the A85.

The Walk

Non-identical twins, joined at the waist by a lofty bealach: Ben More (1,174 metres) and Stob Binnein (1,165 metres) must only ever be climbed together; an inseparable pair. Ben More lives up to its name, the 'big mountain'; it doesn't get closer as you approach it, it just gets bigger! From Benmore Farm the mountain is deceptively foreshortened as the unbroken slopes have few features to allow the eye to discern the true scale of the task.

Stob Binnein is the more reclusive and elegant of the twins. Almost as tall as its big brother, Stob Binnein appears in profile to have a bit missing from the top, as if some mythical giant had taken off the summit cone like the top of his boiled egg. This flat summit explains its Gaelic translation, 'peak of the anvil'.

This outing demands full high mountain gear and preparedness. The climb to Ben More is unrelenting; no false summits, no flat sections; you start at the bottom and keep climbing until you reach the top. On the summit no one to the south in the UK is higher than you, and it will feel like that too! After Ben More we will sweep down a steep slope, losing 312 metres in height, before climbing all the way back up to reach the summit of Stob Binnein. Once we have enjoyed the views it is back down again to the bealach before dropping to the west and heading home. This route involves over 1,200 metres of ascent on rough terrain. In bad weather this is a high and exposed ridge, so go when the forecast is good. The views from both summits are breathtakingly wonderful, that is if you have any breath left after the slog up Ben More!

BEN MORE & STOB BINNEIN

DISTANCE: 9.6KM/6 MILES » **TOTAL ASCENT**: 1,272M/4,173FT » **START GR**: NN 414259 » **TIME**: ALLOW 6-8 HOURS
SATNAV: FK20 8QS » **MAP**: OS EXPLORER OL46, THE TROSSACHS, 1:25,000 » **REFRESHMENTS**: THE ROD AND REEL OR BEN MORE LODGE, CRIANLARICH; ARTISAN CAFE, TYNDRUM » **NAVIGATION**: GOOD PATHS ON HIGH MOUNTAIN TERRAIN.

Directions – Ben More & Stob Binnein

S From the road look for a sign to *Ben More*. Go up to a fence and **go through a gate**. **Turn left** on to a track. Follow the track as it winds steeply up the hillside. **Cross a stile at a gate** and 100m further on look for the start of a new hill path.

2 Go up the stone staircase heading **right** (south-east) across the broad and steep north-west ridge of Ben More. The path is incomplete, but the route is obvious; if you are in any doubt, the direction is up!

3 Reach the remains of a small drystone wall high on the north-west ridge. Follow the path more or less **straight ahead**. Wind through some rocky ground and **trend gradually left**, through steep boulders and small crags. Now head **north** on open hillside and slightly less step terrain. At some big boulders and slabs the path turns **right** and the gradient eases off ... almost there.

4 Cross a flat section towards the summit trig point which sits high on a crag. Scramble up to the summit and take in the views. Your next objective fills the foreground to the south and the entire route up Stob Binnein is clearly visible. If it is cold, wet or windy there is a slot in the summit block beneath the trig point to the west of the summit – a good place to shelter.

5 Take the path heading **south** from the summit and after 100m or so look for a fork in the path above a steep wall. This wall needs a steep **downclimb** of about 3m, down and to the **right** (west) before the path trends **left** down to the bealach. (**To avoid the downclimb**, follow a path above the wall to the **left** (east). This bypasses the scramble then swings back **right** to join up with the other route.) Steep open slopes lead down to Bealach-eadar-dha Bheinn. The bealach is broad and flat with a big erratic boulder near its western edge. This boulder is a good place for shelter and a rest.

6 Head **south** up a good path towards the summit of Stob Binnein. It is steep, but height is gained more easily here than on the slopes of Ben More. At the large summit cairn let's have a look at the views. To the north, look back to Ben More; rotating clockwise we can see the Ben Lawers range. To the east are the distant Perthshire Ben Vorlich and Stùc a'Chroin, then on to Stirling and the Ochil Hills, perhaps with smoke rising from Grangemouth Refinery near Edinburgh. Looking south, the ridge of

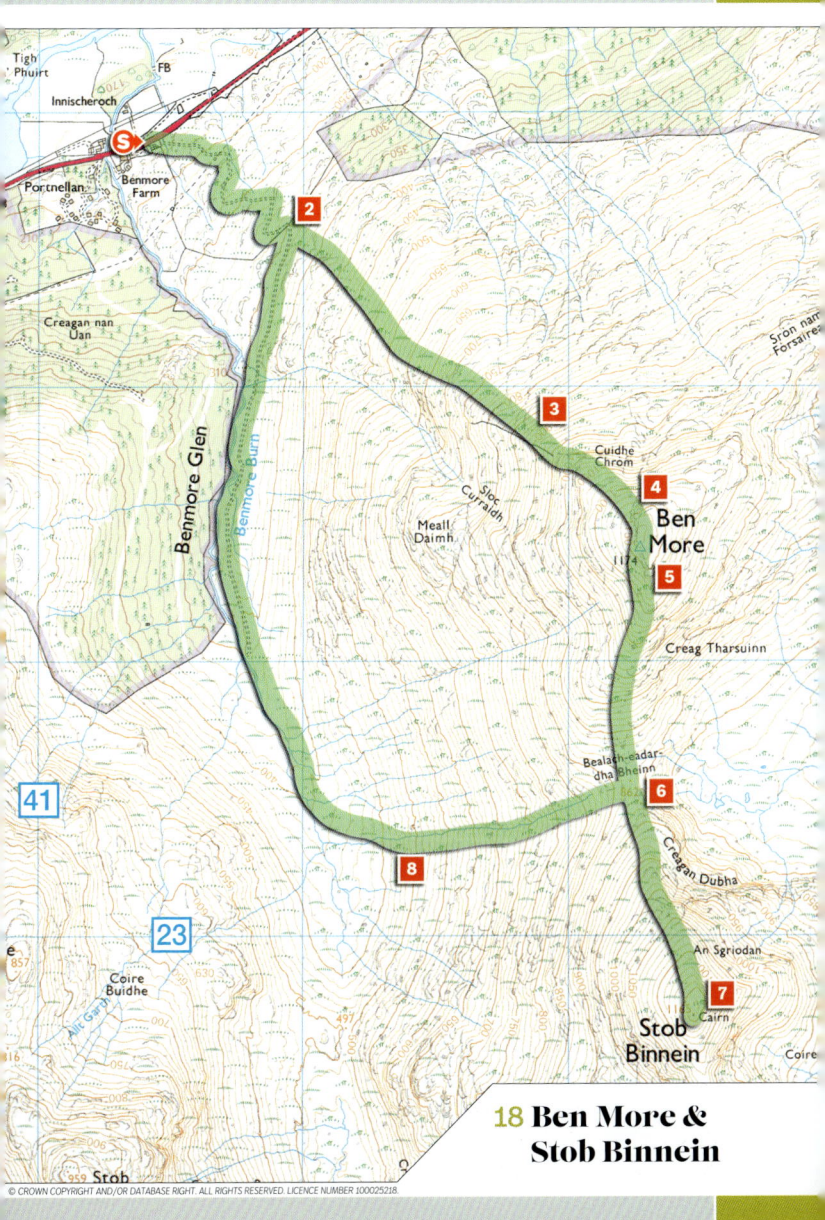

18 Ben More & Stob Binnein

Directions – Ben More & Stob Binnein continued …

Stob Binnein sweeps down over Stob Coire an Lochain to the Braes of Balquhidder. We swing past the Crianlarich Munros and Cruach Ardrain, then to the north-west the top of Ben Lui is sticking out above Ben Oss and Beinn Dubhchraig. Rotate to our starting point past Beinn Chaorach above Tyndrum, then Beinn Challuim, just beyond Strath Fillan far below.

7 **Retrace your steps** to Bealach-eadar-dha Bheinn and the big boulder. At the bealach look **left** (west) to see two faint path systems (one heads diagonally across the western slopes of Ben More and the other one heads straight down the western slopes beside a burn). **Descend the path by the burn.** Start down, steeply at first, **keeping the stream to your right**. Pass the scar of a fairly recent landslide halfway down.

8 Carry on down turning **slightly right**. Soon we can see the track in Benmore Glen. As the path levels, cross a wide piste in the bog and head **north-west** across tussocks to gain the **track**. Once on the track it is a 'hands in pockets' stroll back to where it all started on the way up Ben More. We have earned our supper today!

Notes: These are big mountains so check the forecast thoroughly before you go. The Ben More webcam is also well worth a look **www.benmorewebcam.co.uk** Winter comes early here and lingers late; if there is snow on the hill this is a mountaineering expedition.

BEN MORE AND STOB BINNEIN

STEPS ON BEN MORE

THE START OF THE PATH TO AN CAISTEAL

19 An Caisteal

10.5km/6.5 miles

Storming the citadel!

A82 » Gate » Sròn Gharbh » Twistin Hill » The Castle » An Caisteal summit » The Castle » Twistin Hill » Sròn Gharbh » Gate » A82

Start
Large lay-by on the south side of the A82, 2.5km south of Crianlarich. Busy in high summer. GR: NN 369239.

The Walk
Just beyond the head of Loch Lomond to the north lies a wild tract of land packed with Munros – a feast for the collector of cairns and trig points. These summits can be 'bagged' in big, long days or picked off one at a time. Sometimes the big, long day approach leaves us with little more than memories of sore feet and fatigue. So, our outing for today is just a taster for the Crianlarich Munros, out and back to the most central of summits.

An Caisteal, or as an old shepherd, who was spreading feed on a cold, snowy winter morning, once said to me, as I set off alone, through his hill flock, 'aye, well, you off up Ben an Castle?' Ben an Castle; An Caisteal; the peak of the Castle. The name does not imply that there is, or ever was, a castle on the hill. It refers to the appearance of a castle in outline on the mountain. On any clear day, looking east from the A82 into the middle of the range, we can see the squat rocky battlements of An Caisteal. It is not a big castle, but it is well defended and occupies the high ground.

All mountains have a character of their own and some always want to put up a fight. I can honestly say that, in all my many ascents, I have never climbed An Caisteal in fine or settled weather. I only know the Castle in wind and storm. Maybe you will be luckier?

AN CAISTEAL
DISTANCE: 10.5KM/6.5 MILES » **TOTAL ASCENT**: 826M/2,710FT » **START GR**: NN 369239 » **TIME**: ALLOW 6 HOURS
SATNAV: FK20 8RL » **MAP**: OS EXPLORER OL39, LOCH LOMOND NORTH, 1:25,000 » **REFRESHMENTS**: THE ROD AND REEL OR BEN MORE LODGE, CRIANLARICH; THE DROVERS INN, INVERARNAN » **NAVIGATION**: TRACK THEN ROUGH HILL PATHS; SOME EASY SCRAMBLING.

Directions – An Caisteal

S At the northern (Crianlarich) end of the lay-by, go through the gate and follow the path to the cattle creep beneath the railway line. Cross a bridge over the River Falloch and head south-east on the broad track. Resist the temptation to strike off across the hillside towards Sròn Gharbh. Continue for around 1.5km to a gate. Look for the faint path starting up and **right** (south-west) around 1m after the gate. It is important not to miss this faint path as it avoids a lot of rougher bog-trotting.

2 Go up and steadily **left** across the hillside. It is wet and boggy. Take time to enjoy the views back towards Glen Falloch. The path crosses some rocky slabs then goes up and **right** towards Sròn Gharbh. To our left is the scar of a large landslide. Slope release landslips are becoming more common in these hills due in part to increasingly wet winters. The path, initially broad and indistinct, now becomes rocky and more defined. A short steep climb takes us on to the ridge of Twistin Hill.

3 Head south along the ridge. On a clear day we can see the Castle up ahead. Pass a small buttress which is a good place to shelter from the wind and put on another layer for the summit ridge. The path now crosses a shallow corrie bowl then heads steeply up and **right** on eroded slopes. The Castle is getting closer.

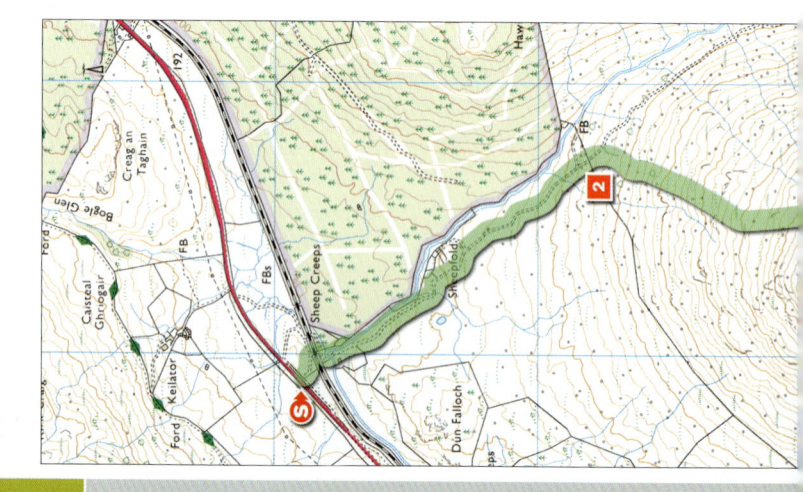

4 Just before the Castle we cross a deep cleft very like a miniature version of the **downclimb** on Ben Donich (walk 13). Follow the path up across a small rocky step then enjoy some short-lived, easy **scrambling** on polished schist slabs – the battlements! The summit of the Castle is marked with a small cairn. The true summit is a few hundred metres further to the south and also has a cairn. Continue along the ridge of the Castle, climb easily down and go up to the true summit of An Caisteal. Time to enjoy the panorama (assuming we are not storm bound!). Let's start with our close neighbour Beinn Chabhair to the south-west. Moving clockwise, in the distance is Beinn Ime and, much closer, is Garabal Hill above Inverarnan. Around across Glen Falloch lie Ben Lui, Beinn Dubhchraig and the 'gold mine' hill – Beinn a'Chuirn. Continuing on, we cross Strath Fillan in the north-west and pick out the distant Beinn Chaorach and a sharply pointed Beinn Challuim. Views to the north are the ridges of Cruach Adrain, Ben More, Stob Binnein, Beinn Tulaichean and then, our nearest neighbour, Beinn a'Chroin. We're now back to the starting point; we have lots to plan for other days.

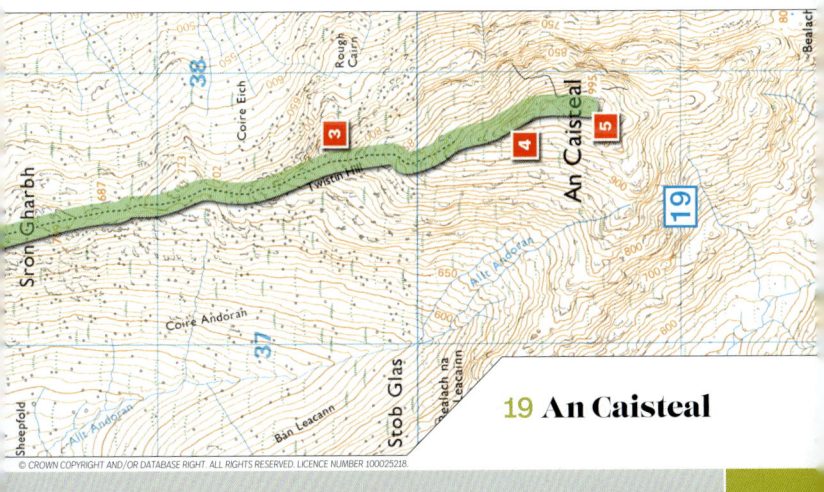

19 An Caisteal

Directions – An Caisteal continued ...

5 We **retrace our steps** to descend. If it is windy or wet the **scrambling section on the Castle can be avoided** by a short detour to the **left** (west). Head down the path then go **diagonally left** across steep grassy slopes below and west of the Castle. This detour goes beneath the Castle with good, sheltered spots for a lunch stop. **Don't go too far to the left** as a boulderfield makes the walking difficult. Once beyond the Castle, contour back up and **right** to regain the main path just before the deep cleft. Follow the route all the way back to the bealach before Sròn Gharbh then head down and **right** to the track at the gate. **Turn left** along the track to return to the start.

Notes: This could easily be combined with an ascent of Beinn a'Chroin, descending over Stob Glas Bheag before returning to the track via pathless terrain in Coire Earb. Another option is to descend via the ridge of Stob Glas to the west before heading north on pathless terrain beneath Sròn Gharbh to return to the start point. Lots of options, depending on weather and how energetic you feel!

A WALKER ENJOYING AN CAISTEAL

TWISTIN HILL

LOCH EARN FROM BEN VORLICH

20 Ben Vorlich & Stùc a'Chroin   14.2km/8.8 miles

A high mountain circuit with an optional scramble on Stùc a'Chroin.

Ardvorlich House » Glen Vorlich » Ben Vorlich » Bealach an Dubh Choirein » Stùc a'Chroin » Coire Fhuadaraich » Coire Buidhe » Glen Vorlich » Ardvorlich House

Start
Limited roadside parking near Ardvorlich House, Loch Earn. GR: NN 632232.

The Walk

Loch Lomond & the Trossachs National Park has two Munros called Ben Vorlich. 'Vorlich' means peak of the bay or inlet. This Vorlich's bay is on Loch Earn in the far north-east corner of the national park. This is a circuit of Ben Vorlich and its neighbour, Stùc a'Chroin. These two Munros tower above the surrounding terrain and are easily seen from the south, especially when travelling on the A9 between Perth and Stirling. Ben Vorlich presents a smooth, whaleback outline with a long summit ridge. Worthy of the term 'Stùc', meaning pointed or steep, Stùc a'Chroin stands just 1.9 kilometres away to the south-west.

Leaving the shores of Loch Earn we follow wide, easy paths all the way to the summit of Ben Vorlich. Stùc a'Chroin, by contrast, is an altogether more rugged experience. The Stùc requires us to tackle rough, steep ground and to get our hands out of our pockets. On the way down we will navigate across a wild corrie to regain the good paths we used in ascent.

For some, Ben Vorlich might be plenty. Others will want to visit both summits, but the steep scramble up Stùc a'Chroin is not for everyone, so an optional route is described to miss this out if needed. So there really is something for everyone on this outing.

BEN VORLICH & STÙC A'CHROIN

DISTANCE: 14.2KM/8.8 MILES » **TOTAL ASCENT**: 1,130M/3,707FT » **START GR**: NN 632232 » **TIME**: ALLOW 6–8 HOURS
SATNAV: FK19 8QE » **MAP**: OS EXPLORER OL46, THE TROSSACHS, 1:25,000 » **REFRESHMENTS**: NONE NEARBY
NAVIGATION: HIGH MOUNTAIN TERRAIN; GOOD PATHS, SOME EASY SCRAMBLING.

Directions – Ben Vorlich & Stùc a'Chroin

S **Walk through the gateway** of Ardvorlich House. A few metres west of the gates, a stone marks the burial site of seven McDonald clansmen killed in a raid in the 17th century. Walk along the broad driveway following signs to the hill. **Go through a gate** and up the track heading **south** into Glen Vorlich. Climb through mixed woodlands, cross some fords and go through numerous gates. **Ignore** a path heading left (east). Follow the main track up and **right** to a bridge and a small hydro dam.

2 **Cross the bridge**; the path goes up open hillside with the entire route up Ben Vorlich visible ahead. The path is easy to the foot of the north ridge.

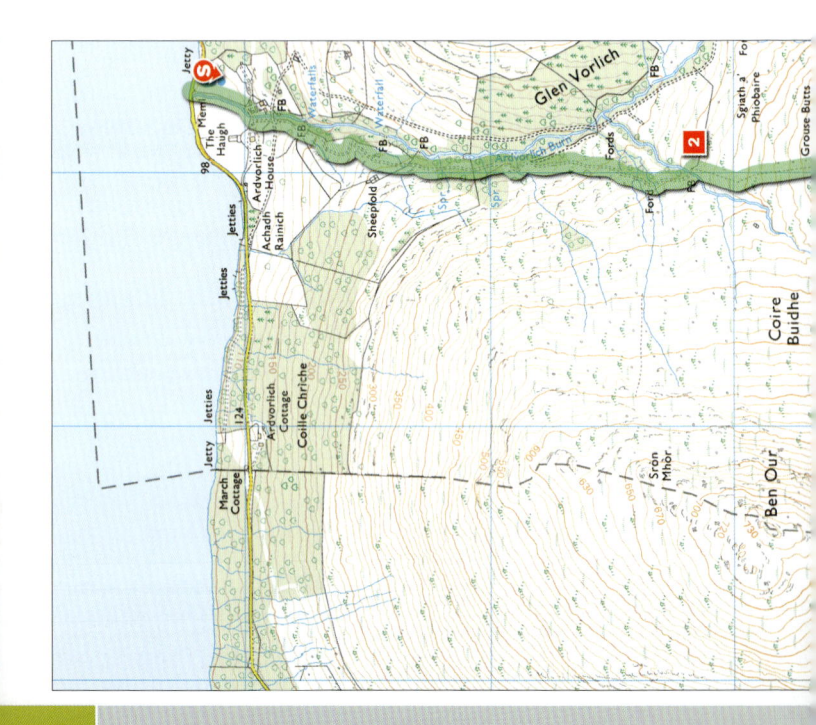

3 The path now becomes **eroded and rocky** as it climbs up and **left to a flat area** marked with a cairn. This is a favourite spot for ravens to soar in the updrafts. Follow the track up past another cairn and then a **broad flat area** just below the final summit push.

4 We can now see the trig point as the path winds up and **left**, hugging the edge of the corrie. The summit is a narrow, level ridge with a trig point at the western end; this is the true summit but only by a metre or so. At the eastern end a cairn sits on rocks and just below this, on the northern side, is a nice little natural shelter in the rocks. The views are super, but those from our next objective are probably better. Until now we haven't seen our next summit, so let's go find it.

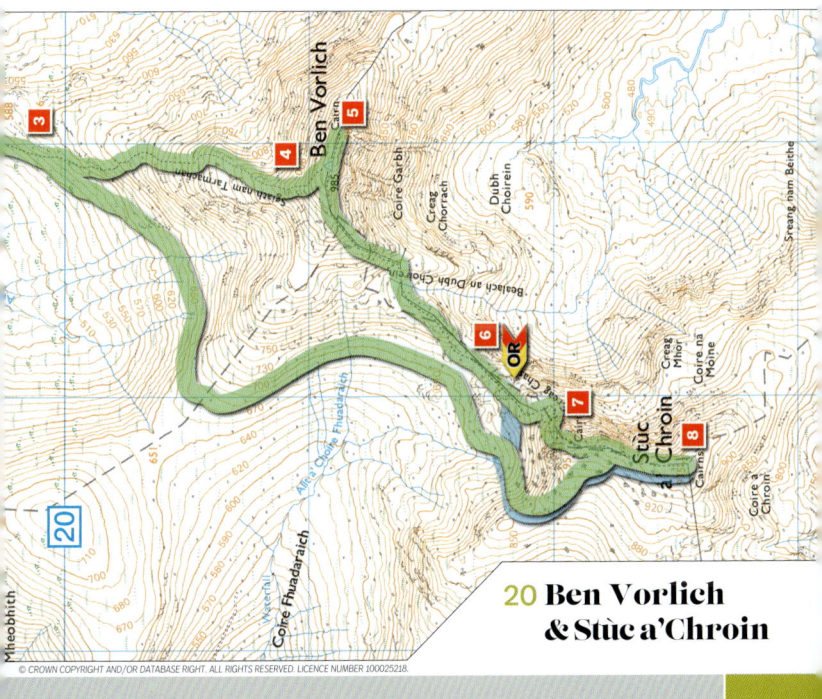

20 Ben Vorlich & Stùc a'Chroin

Directions – Ben Vorlich & Stùc a'Chroin continued ...

5 Go back along the summit ridge to the trig point. (If you have had enough, just go back down the ascent route and settle for Ben Vorlich, no shame in that is there? However, Stùc a'Chroin is nearby and it would be a shame to miss out.) Just beyond the trig point follow a narrow path **west** then go **left (south-west)** and descend steeply to the Bealach an Dubh Choirein. Follow the path down, winding around rocky buttresses. Some old iron fenceposts mark the way and dead ahead rises the rocky summit cone of the Stùc. It looks very steep and rocky, which it is!

6 While the direct route is steep, it follows a narrow path and only requires us to scramble short, easy sections. It is important to **stick to the path** here. **Leave the southern end of the bealach at its eastern edge**. The path enters a boulderfield and is difficult to follow. Go up and **right** out of the boulderfield to a narrow path up through easy rocks. Climb up and **right** (west) on a narrow ledge. A short vertical corner is tackled head on, with big holds leading to another ledge. Head up and **left** (east) over two more steep scrambles to reach the flat, northern fore-summit. Phew!

> **OR** To **avoid the scrambling section** near the top of Stùc a'Chroin, **leave the path** just below the steep crags (NN 620182) and go **west** heading for the wide corrie at NN 617182. Go up the broad, steep and eroded path to reach the summit plateau just west of the crags then head up and **east** to regain the easy path leading to the true summit. Follow **8** to return to the start.

7 The true summit of Stùc a'Chroin lies 500m to the **south** and is marked by two cairns, the eastern one is highest. The views are well worth the effort so let's have a look. To the north, we can see Ben Vorlich's rugged southern face. Moving clockwise, we see Ben Chonzie then the eye is drawn down Gleann an Dubh Choirein to the flat lands of the east. Further south are the Touch Hills south of Stirling, then Ben Ledi, the Crianlarich Hills and Ben More and Stob Binnein. Then it is across to the Glen Lochay Munros and back towards our start point lies the nearby Lawers Range. With so much low ground to the south and east, the views are really special.

8 We can avoid the steep scrambling route by descending to the upper reaches of Coire Fhuadaraich. Retrace our steps **north** from the summit for **250m** then go **left** (west) to a track leading down to a broad notch on the north-west ridge of Stùc a'Chroin. Beyond the notch take the path steeply down on slippery ground and head **north** into the corrie below the summit cone of the Stùc. Follow the broad muddy trail **north** across the corrie, towards another **bealach** on the north-west ridge of Ben Vorlich. **Cross this ridge** then head **north-east** above a line of white wooden stakes, around the upper reaches of Coire Buidhe. This is muddy and rough but soon leads to the main path. **Turn left** and head back down the trail to Ardvorlich House.

Notes: The scrambling section is entirely avoidable by the Coire Fhuadaraich optional route. In bad weather or poor visibility this is a serious outing and of course in winter it is an expedition.

LEDGES LEADING TO THE SCRAMBLING SECTION ON STÙC A'CHROIN

Appendix

VISITOR INFORMATION CENTRES
www.lochlomond-trossachs.org

Aberfoyle	T: **01877 381 221**
Balloch	T: **01389 753 533**
Balmaha	T: **01389 722 100**
Duke's Pass	T: **03000 676 615**
Glen Finglas	T: **01877 376 340**

FOOD AND DRINK

There are too many cafes, restaurants, bars, inns and hotels to list but a quick web search before you go will whet the appetite. In peak season, the major national park centres such as Balmaha, Callander, Arrochar, Crianlarich, Luss and Balloch all have lots to choose from.

ACCOMMODATION
www.visitscotland.com

www.hostellingscotland.org.uk

Wild Camping

Wild camping within the national park boundary is strictly regulated and policed in the summer, so paradoxically if you want to wild camp in some areas you may need a permit; see **www.lochlomond-trossachs.org**

WEATHER
www.mwis.org.uk

www.metoffice.gov.uk

www.smidgeup.com/midge-forecast

PUBLIC TRANSPORT
www.citylink.co.uk

www.scotrail.co.uk

www.lochlomond-trossachs.org

OTHER PUBLICATIONS

Day Walks in Fort William & Glen Coe
Helen & Paul Webster, Vertebrate Publishing
www.v-publishing.co.uk

Day Walks in the Cairngorms
Helen & Paul Webster, Vertebrate Publishing
www.v-publishing.co.uk

Day Walks in Northumberland
David Wilson, Vertebrate Publishing
www.v-publishing.co.uk

Classic Day Walks in England & Wales
Edited by Jon Barton, Vertebrate Publishing
www.v-publishing.co.uk

Big Trails: Great Britain & Ireland
Edited by Kathy Rogers & Stephen Ross, Vertebrate Publishing
www.v-publishing.co.uk

West Highland Way Guidemap
Vertebrate Publishing
www.v-publishing.co.uk

Scottish Island Bagging
Helen & Paul Webster, Vertebrate Publishing
www.v-publishing.co.uk

Traffic-Free Cycle Trails
Nick Cotton, Vertebrate Publishing
www.v-publishing.co.uk

DOUNE HILL (ROUTE 5)

GLEN LOIN (ROUTE 12)

APPENDIX

Day Walks Guidebooks

Written by local authors, each pocket-sized guidebook features:

- 20 great day-length walks
- Ordnance Survey 1:25,000-scale maps
- easy-to-follow directions
- distance & navigation information
- refreshment stops & local area information
- detailed appendix

1. Day Walks in the Cairngorms
2. Day walks in Fort William & Glen Coe
3. Day walks in Loch Lomond & the Trossachs
4. Day Walks in Snowdonia
5. Day Walks in the Brecon Beacons
6. Day Walks on the Pembrokeshire Coast
7. Day Walks in the Lake District
8. Day Walks in Northumberland
9. Day Walks in the Yorkshire Dales
10. Day Walks in the North York Moors
11. Day Walks in the South Pennines
12. Day Walks in the Peak District
13. Day Walks in the Peak District
14. Day Walks in East Anglia
15. Day Walks in the Cotswolds
16. Day Walks in Devon
17. Day Walks in Cornwall
18. Day Walks on the High Weald
19. Day Walks on the South Downs

Available from book shops or direct from
www.v-publishing.co.uk

20% off!

More great titles from
Vertebrate Publishing

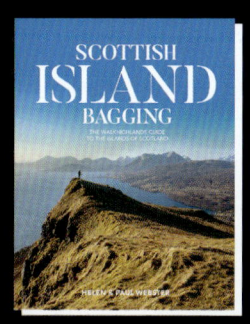

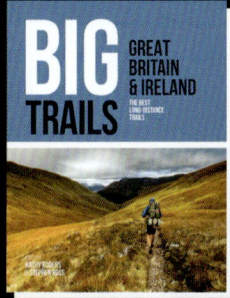

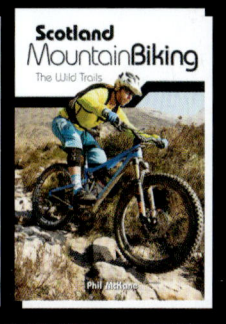

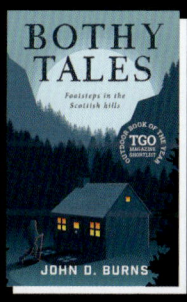

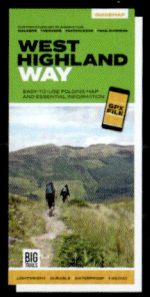

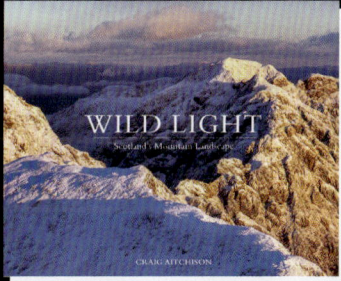

- SCOTTISH ISLAND BAGGING
- BIG TRAILS — GREAT BRITAIN & IRELAND
- Scotland Mountain Biking: The Wild Trails
- BOTHY TALES — John D. Burns
- WEST HIGHLAND WAY
- WILD LIGHT — Scotland's Mountain Landscape

vp inspiring adventure

Available direct with
20% off and free UK P&P
www.v-publishing.co.uk

ABOUT THE AUTHOR

Gerald McGarry has been a keen hillwalker and climber for many years. He has mountaineered extensively throughout Scotland, the Alps and in five of the seven continents (so far!). In a busy professional career every spare moment was spent in the great outdoors. When Gerald isn't hillwalking, climbing or complaining about the lack of Scottish ice, he can be found on his paddleboard or kayak or having a swim at his home beside Loch Lomond.

VERTEBRATE PUBLISHING

At Vertebrate Publishing we publish books to inspire adventure.

It's our rule that the only books we publish are those that we'd want to read or use ourselves. We endeavour to bring you beautiful books that stand the test of time and that you'll be proud to have on your bookshelf for years to come.

The Peak District was the inspiration behind our first books. Our offices are situated on its doorstep, minutes away from world-class climbing, biking and hillwalking. We're driven by our own passion for the outdoors, for exploration, and for the natural world; it's this passion that we want to share with our readers.

We aim to inspire everyone to get out there. We want to connect readers – young and old – with the outdoors and the positive impact it can have on well-being. We think it's particularly important that young people get outside and explore the natural world, something we support through our publishing programme.

As well as publishing award-winning new books, we're working to make available many out-of-print classics in both print and digital formats. These are stories that we believe are unique and significant; we want to make sure that they continue to be shared and enjoyed.
www.v-publishing.co.uk